FIRESIDE CHATS

(VOLUME ONE)

TEACHER'S GUIDE

TakingITGlobal
INSPIRE INFORM INVOLVE

Connected North

CONTENTS

GENERAL LESSONS

Indigenous Careers Inquiry Project 4

Indigenous Role Model Presentation 13

COMPUTER SCIENCE **20**

Lesson One: Dallas Storm Flett-Wapash 20

Lesson Two: Ashlee Foureyes 28

CULTURE **33**

Lesson One: Joy Hall 33

Lesson Two: Curtis Clearsky 41

Lesson Three: Carly Chartier 56

SKILLED TRADES **68**

Lesson One: Sateana Goupil 68

Lesson Two: Raven Beardy 74

Lesson Three: Krista Paul 79

ELECTED OFFICIALS **85**

Lesson One: Mumilaaq Qaqqaq 85

Lesson Two: Senator Yvonne Boyer 94

HEALTH AND SCIENCE **104**

Lesson One: Taylar Belanger 104

Lesson Two: Pihêsiw Crane 113

Lesson Three: James Harper 121

ENTERTAINMENT **126**

Lesson One: Evan Redsky 126

Lesson Two: Dakota Bear 132

ARTS   138

Lesson One: Monique (Mo) Aura Bedard   138

Lesson Two: Hanwakan Blakie Whitecloud   143

Lesson Three: Nooks Lindell   147

SPORT AND RECREATION   152

Lesson One: Carson Roche   152

Lesson Two: Richard Pellissier-Lush   155

BUSINESS AND ENTREPRENEURSHIP   158

Lesson One: Jessica Dumas   158

Lesson Two: Dana Marlatt   165

EDUCATION   169

Lesson One: Brianna Oversby   169

Lesson Two: Christine M'Lot   175

Lesson Three: Niigaan Sinclair   180

Lesson Four: Dr. Glen Sharpe   188

COMMUNITY DEVELOPMENT   192

Lesson One: Diane Roussin   192

Lesson Two: Reanna Merasty   198

TakingITGlobal
117 Peter Street, Suite 212
Toronto, Ontario
M5V 0M3

Copyright © 2021 by TakingITGlobal

ISBN: 978-0-578-32175-2 (paperback)

Produced with the Financial Support of the RBC Foundation & Government of
Canada's Supports for Student Learning program

Written by Christine M'lot and Marika Schalla/Waabishkaanakwadikwe

Cover illustrations by Shaikara David, Akwesasne Mohawk Territory

www.firesidechats.ca

In the early days of the COVID-19 pandemic, TakingITGlobal's Connected North program launched the Fireside Chats initiative to develop inspiring videos about education and career pathways for students to access at home. The web site (www.firesidechats.ca) has now grown into a home for more than 100 videos, articles and illustrations made possible through funding from RBC Foundation in support of RBC Future Launch.

This teacher guide includes fully developed lesson plans to accompany our first volume of Fireside Chat interviews with First Nations, Métis, and Inuit role models. Through these lesson plans, students will explore the career journeys of inspiring Indigenous leaders and engage in learning activities to increase their understanding of the diverse career categories discussed in the videos. Career categories explored in this teacher guide include Activism, Arts/Graphic Arts, Business and Entrepreneurship, Community Development, Computer Science, Culture, Education, Entertainment, Government, Health and Science, Skilled Trades, and Sports and Recreation.

These lessons are best suited for use in Grade 8 – 12 classrooms, and many of the lesson are cross curricular – bridging subjects such as English Language Arts, Indigenous Studies, Art/Graphic Arts, Social Studies, Mathematics, Entrepreneurship, Marketing, Computer Science and more! At the beginning of each lesson, we've included course connections for Alberta, British Columbia, Northwest Territories, Nunavut, Ontario, and Yukon.

The lesson plans are formatted using the AAAA format. *Activating* activities will assess students' prior knowledge and pique students' interest in the topic. *Acquire* activities involve students watching the *Fireside Chat* interview either individually or together as a class. During the *apply* section, students will demonstrate their learning through a variety of engaging and relevant learning activities. The final section - *assessment* - includes several examples of formative and summative assessment options. Each lesson also includes all supplementary materials such as handouts and rubrics. Some lessons include a section called *Take Learning Further*, in which we provide extension activities if students would like to deepen their understanding of the topic.

Since the Fireside Chat interviews provide students with a sense of Indigenous cultural pride, it was important to us to include Indigenous learning processes throughout. Examples of Indigenous learning processes included in this guide are engaging in respectful dialogue (sometimes in the form of a sharing circle), learning from local Elders/Knowledge keepers, learning through the land, storytelling, and creating projects that give back to the community.

We hope your students are inspired through each lesson!

Jennifer Corriero, Executive Director

Michael Furdyk, Director of Innovation

Christine M'Iot, Educator & Lead Author

Marika Schalla, Educator and Co-author

TakingITGlobal is honoured to have collaborated with educators Christine M'lot and Marika Schalla to develop this resource with their knowledge and expertise.

Christine M'Lot (she/her) is an Anishinaabe educator and curriculum developer from Winnipeg, Manitoba. She has experience working with children and youth in multiple capacities including child welfare, children's disability services, and Indigenous family programming. She currently teaches high school at the University of Winnipeg Collegiate. Christine is also the co-founder of Red Rising Education and works to create Indigenous education resources for teachers.

Marika Schalla/Waabishkaanakwadikwe, (she/her) is an early years educator, student, curriculum developer, and mother of two. Marika is an Indigenous Red River Métis and Anishinaabkwe, from Winnipeg, Manitoba. Marika holds a Bachelor of Science in Biology and a Bachelor of Education. She is currently completing her Post-Baccalaureate Diploma in Education in Indigenous Knowledges. Marika has a passion for Earth-based education and integrating Indigenous knowledges and pedagogies in the classroom. She strives to cause real change in our school systems. Her work reflects meaningful reconciliation that engages our Indigenous and non-Indigenous youth and provides them with Indigenous cultural and traditional connections, knowledges, perspectives, and opportunities to make a difference.

General Lesson Plan One

CURRICULUM CONNECTIONS	**Alberta, Northwest Territories and Nunavut:**

Alberta, Northwest Territories and Nunavut:
- English Language Arts 10, 20, 30
- Knowledge and Employability English Language Arts 10, 20, 30
- Career and Technology Foundations Grade 9
- Career and Technology Studies 10, 20, 30
- Entrepreneurship 11, 12

British Columbia and Yukon:
- Entrepreneurship and Marketing 10
- Career Life Education 10, 11, 12
- Career Life Connections 10,11, 12
- English Language Arts 10, 11, 12

Ontario:
- Career Studies Grade 10
- First Nations, Metis and Inuit Studies Grades 9-12
- Business Studies Grades 9-10
- Business Studies Grade 11-12
- English Language Arts Grades 9-10
- English Language Arts Grades 11-12

DURATION

2-3 hours *(One class for inquiry, 1-2 classes for presentations)*

OVERVIEW

Students will learn and explore career opportunities that are available in various Indigenous career sectors. Indigenous careers can involve jobs from numerous sectors, including health care, education, business, arts, and more. Indigenous jobs sectors are typical "every-day" jobs that either include some form of Indigenous cultural aspect or impact an Indigenous community. A person working in the Indigenous jobs sector can work in an Indigenous organization, community, business; work as an Indigenous person; work with Indigenous peoples; or work in a job that they can attain with an Indigenous Studies post-secondary education. Indigenous careers are important to Canada and our economy so there are many Indigenous communities and organizations that offer such employment. Students who may not even be aware of the plethora of careers and opportunities offered in the Indigenous job sector. Learning about various Indigenous careers contributes to the spirit of reconciliation by teaching both Indigenous and non-Indigenous students the positive impacts that Indigenous careers have on our community. Students will research a career that is highlighted in a chosen Fireside Chats video series. Students will then create a 3-5 minute presentation of their career to the class in their chosen presentation style (poster, PowerPoint presentation, etc.)

MATERIALS

- "Indigenous Career Sector Jobs Opportunities" Reproducible
- "Indigenous Careers Inquiry Project Example"
- "Indigenous Careers Inquiry Template"
- "Indigenous Careers Inquiry Checklist"
- Sticky notes and writing instruments (pencils, pens, etc.)
- Computer and internet access

ACTIVATE: WHAT IS THE "INDIGENOUS JOBS SECTOR"

To begin this lesson, you will pose the question: "If you could have any career you wanted, what would it be?" Do a think-pair-share strategy with your students. Have students silently think of an answer for about a minute. Afterwards, have the students pair off to share their ideas. Provide each pair with a sticky note to write their ideas on. When they are ready to share, students will place their sticky note on the board. The teacher will then read out all the ideas.

Next, pose the question: "Let us think about careers that impact Indigenous peoples, communities, and organizations. What careers do you think would fall under the umbrella of the "Indigenous Jobs Sector"? Have students silently think of their answers again. Pair students off to share their ideas and provide a second sticky note. Partners will write their answers and place their stick note on the board. The teacher will read out all of the ideas.

Instruct students that their answers are all great ideas and share that there are in fact many jobs in the Indigenous Jobs Sector. Most jobs can fall under the Indigenous Jobs Sector! Using the *Indigenous Job Opportunities* Reproducible, share a few of the possible career and job opportunities that are available in the Indigenous jobs sector.

ACQUIRE: FUTURE PATHWAYS FIRESIDE CHATS VIDEOS

Watch a Fireside Chats video of your choosing. To showcase to the class an Indigenous career. There are many interesting videos to show students. Pick one from the list below to show the class as a whole-class example.

Examples:

- Activism/Education: Christine M'Lot, Teacher
- Arts/Graphic Arts: Monique Aura Bedard, Art Maker
- Athletes/Sports and Recreation: Richard Pellissier-Lush, Collegiate Athlete
- Business and Entrepreneurship: Jessica Dumas, Life Coach
- Community Development: Diane Roussin, Non-Profit Project Director
- Computer Science: Dallas Wapash-Flett, Video Game Designer
- Culture: Curtis Clearsky, Food Relations Coordinator
- Elected Officials: Yvonne Boyer, Senator
- Entertainment: Dakota Bear, Hip-Hop Artist and Activist
- Health and Science: Taylar Belanger, Traditional Herbalist
- Skilled Trades: Raven Beardy, Pilot

Debrief the video by asking the class the following questions. Ask students to raise their hands and call upon someone to answer:

1. What career category/job sector is this job from?
2. What was the job highlighted in the video?
3. What kind of education did this role model have?
4. What kind of duties did they have with their job?
5. What impact did this person have on Indigenous peoples and/or communities?

Next, let students choose their own career from the *Fireside Chats Series* Reproducible list to explore. Allow students the opportunity to independently browse all the Fireside Chat videos and pick one that they want to present about: https://www.firesidechats.ca

ACQUIRE: FUTURE PATHWAYS FIRESIDE CHATS VIDEOS

Watch a Fireside Chats video of your choosing. To showcase to the class an Indigenous career.

There are many interesting videos to show students. Pick one from the list below to show the class as a whole-class example.

Examples:

- Activism/Education: Christine M'Lot, Teacher
- Arts/Graphic Arts: Monique Aura Bedard, Art Maker
- Athletes/Sports and Recreation: Richard Pellissier-Lush, Collegiate Athlete
- Business and Entrepreneurship: Jessica Dumas, Life Coach
- Community Development: Diane Roussin, Non-Profit Project Director
- Computer Science: Dallas Wapash-Flett, Video Game Designer
- Culture: Curtis Clearsky, Food Relations Coordinator
- Elected Officials: Yvonne Boyer, Senator
- Entertainment: Dakota Bear, Hip-Hop Artist and Activist
- Health and Science: Taylar Belanger, Traditional Herbalist
- Skilled Trades: Raven Beardy, Pilot

Debrief the video by asking the class the following questions. Ask students to raise their hands and call upon someone to answer:

1. What career category/job sector is this job from?
2. What was the job highlighted in the video?
3. What kind of education did this role model have?
4. What kind of duties did they have with their job?
5. What impact did this person have on Indigenous peoples and/or communities?

Next, let students choose their own career from the *Fireside Chats Series* Reproducible list to explore. Allow students the opportunity to independently browse all the Fireside Chat videos and pick one that they want to present about: https://www.firesidechats.ca

APPLY: INDIGENOUS CAREERS INQUIRY PROJECT

Provide the students with possible resources they may need so they can explore more information related to the career. Provide resources such as websites that may be talked about in the videos, the Canadian Job Bank website, or other online resources if needed.

Show students the *Indigenous Career Inquiry Project Example* detailing the level of research required for this project.

Inform students that they will create their own 3-5 minute presentation on an Indigenous career highlighted in the Fireside Chat series. Students may choose the style of presentation such as a poster or a PowerPoint presentation.

Students will research the following key points:

1. Job Sector
2. Job Overview
3. Educational Requirements
4. Job Duties
5. Impact on Indigenous people/communities
6. Interesting Facts/Information

Students will present their presentations on their Indigenous career to the class. After the presentations discuss the following as a class:

1. Were you surprised by the diversity of careers available in the Indigenous Jobs sector?
2. What makes careers in the Indigenous job sector different from other jobs? The same?

ASSESSMENT

The think-pair-share strategy is a form of formative assessment. Teachers will be able to check students' prior knowledge on the subject and correct misconceptions as they read out the students' answers from the sticky notes.

The inquiry-based research project is a form of summative assessment. Using the checklist provided below to mark students' presentations and provide them with constructive feedback. They can use this feedback for improvement of future presentations. Students will be marked on if their presentation included a clear, concise job overview, if their presentation included the correct job sector, if their presentation included all the educational requirements needed for the career, if their presentation included 5-8 duties of the job, if their presentation clearly reported the impact on Indigenous peoples/communities, and if their presentation included 5-8 interesting facts of the job. Students will also be marked on if their presentation was engaging, and the presenter spoke with appropriate volume and if the presentation was well-organized, easy to follow and was in the 3-5 minute time frame.

The discussion questions are a form of self-assessment. Check for students' new understanding and correct any last misconceptions students may have.

Take Student Learning Further
Activity: Indigenous Job Sector Career Fair

Student learning does not have to stop with their presentations to their class. Students can create tri-fold boards of their research and invite other classrooms down to preview a career fair. Students can teach other classrooms about the many opportunities available in the Indigenous careers sector and how Indigenous peoples make amazing contributions to our communities and economy!

INDIGENOUS CAREERS INQUIRY EXAMPLE

Below is an example of the expectations for the amount of research required for the Indigenous Careers Introduction presentation project. You will need to research each section using both the information in the Fireside Chat and internet research.

Fireside Chat: Christine M'Lot
Career: Indigenous Educator

Job Overview
- An Indigenous Educator is a teacher or administrator that is First Nations, Metis, or Inuit. An Indigenous Educator uses Indigenous knowledge, teachings, histories, methods, and content within their teaching practice.

Job Sector
- An Indigenous Educator works in the Education and Training sector.

Educational Requirements
- An Indigenous Educator needs a high school diploma. As well as a primary bachelor's degree in their choosing. Their first bachelor's degree could be in Arts or Science. Usually Indigenous Educators have Indigenous Studies as a major or minor but, they do not always have to. An Indigenous Educator also needs a second bachelor's degree in Education. A lot of Indigenous Educators go on to get Post-Baccalaureate diplomas in subjects of their choice and/or Master's degrees in education in subjects of their choice.

Job Duties
Indigenous Educators have the same job duties as any other kind of teacher. There are many duties that a teacher has to do. Here is a list of some of the duties of an Indigenous Educator:

- Apply Indigenous knowledges and traditions in the classroom,
- Create lesson plans,
- Teach the curriculum to their students,
- Track student progress and assess students,
- Create assignments, tests, quizzes, and other assessments,
- Create and reinforce classroom rules and expectations,
- Support students with learning new skills and information,
- Provide a safe and inclusive classroom for all learners,
- Manage student behaviour in the classroom.

Impact on Indigenous People/Communities
- By incorporating Indigenous perspectives and knowledge in the classroom Indigenous students are provided with the knowledge that will enable them to participate more meaningfully as citizens in their own cultural communities. Similarly, Non-Indigenous students are provided with the knowledge of the histories, culture, and accomplishments of the Indigenous peoples. They are provided information that supports decolonization. Decolonization in education is a benefit to all students.

Interesting Facts about this Career
1. There are many Indigenous educators who include their own language in their classroom in some format.
2. Some Indigenous educators may not know much about their own culture, and that is okay!
3. Indigenizing a classroom and decolonizing a classroom are similar but different concepts.
4. Many Indigenous educators like to work in their home communities. Giving back to the community where they grow up or connect the most to.
5. Indigenous education looks different all across Canada because, there are so many different traditions, perspectives, and knowledges based on various groups and nations.

INDIGENOUS CAREERS INQUIRY TEMPLATE

Use the template below to help with your research for the Indigenous Careers Inquiry presentation.

Student Name: _____

Fireside Chat: _____

Career: _____

Job Sector
What job sector is this career a part of?

_____

_____

Job Overview
A job overview describes the career. Who has this career? What do they do?
Write at least 5-8 sentences for this section.

_____

_____

_____

_____

_____

_____

_____

_____

_____

_____

_____

_____

_____

Educational Requirements
What kind of education does one need to attain to have this career? Can they do this job directly out of high school? Apprenticeship? Postsecondary?
Write at least 3-4 sentences for this section.

_____

_____

_____

Job Duties

There might be many duties and tasks that someone needs to complete at their job.

In this section list at least 5-8 duties of the job.

1. _____

2. _____

3. _____

4. _____

5. _____

6. _____

7. _____

8. _____

Impact on Indigenous People/Communities

Who and what are they working with? How does this job impact Indigenous peoples or Indigenous communities? Write 5-8 sentences for this section.

_____

_____

_____

_____

_____

Interesting Facts about this Career

There might be interesting, fascinating, or astounding facts you have learned about this career while doing your inquiry. In this section you can list 5-8 interesting facts.

1. _____

2. _____

3. _____

4. _____

5. _____

6. _____

7. _____

8. _____

INDIGENOUS CAREER SECTOR JOB OPPORTUNITIES

This is a non-exhaustive list of job and career opportunities examples a person can have in an Indigenous organization, community, as an Indigenous person, working with Indigenous peoples.

Elected Officials/Politics Sector:
- Indigenous Governance
- Chief
- Politician
- Lawyer
- Senator
- Member of Parliament

Arts/Graphic Sector:
- Art Maker
- Art Therapist
- Filmmaker
- Designer
- Creative Lead

Skilled Trades Sector:
- Electrician
- Hair stylist
- Pilot
- Makeup Artist

Business & Entrepreneurship Sector:
- Indigenous Social Entrepreneurship
- Indigenous Liaison
- Non-Profit Organizations
- Human Resources

Community Development/Youth Engagement Sector:
- Community Development Worker
- Family Support Worker
- Indigenous Outreach Worker
- Cultural Coordinator
- Social Worker
- Aboriginal Youth Opportunities
- Child and Family Services Worker

Computer Science Sector:
- Game Designer
- Interactive Media Specialist
- Software Engineer

Culture Sector:
- Vegetable Farmer
- Food Relations Coordinator
- Friendship Centre Administrator
- Knowledge Keeper
- Elder
- Traditional Herbalist

Activism Sector:
- Activist
- Action Therapist
- Youth Mentor
- Program Coordinator
- Kairos Blanket Exercise Facilitator

Education Sector:
- Indigenous Educator
- University Instructor
- Language Teacher
- Educational Consult

Entertainment Sector:
- Actor/Actress
- Writer
- Singer/Songwriter
- Dancer
- Model
- Social Media Influence

Health and Science Sector:
- Indigenous Medicines Doctor
- Doula
- Therapist
- Community Health Nurse
- Addictions Counselling
- Traditional Herbalist
- Indigenous Forestry Sector
- Engineer

Athletes/Sports and Recreation Sector:
- Hockey player
- Program Coordinator
- Football player

INDIGENOUS CAREERS INQUIRY CHECKLIST

Student Name: _____

0 NO	1 SOMEWHAT	2 YES	
☐	☐	☐	Presentation included a clear, concise job overview.
☐	☐	☐	Presentation included the correct job sector.
☐	☐	☐	Presentation included all the educational requirements needed for the career.
☐	☐	☐	Presentation included 5-8 duties of the job.
☐	☐	☐	Presentation clearly reported the impact on Indigenous peoples/communities.
☐	☐	☐	Presentation included 5-8 interesting facts of the job.
☐	☐	☐	The presentation was engaging, and the presenter spoke with appropriate volume.
☐	☐	☐	The presentation was well-organized, easy to follow and was in the 3-5 minute time frame.

Total = _____ out of 16

Teacher Feedback:

General Lesson Plan Two

Activity: Indigenous Role Model Presentation

CURRICULUM
CONNECTIONS

Alberta, Northwest Territories and Nunavut:

- English Language Arts 10, 20, 30
- Knowledge and Employability English Language Arts 10, 20, 30
- Career and Technology Foundations Grade 9
- Career and Technology Studies 10, 20, 30
- Entrepreneurship 11, 12

British Columbia and Yukon:

- Entrepreneurship and Marketing 10
- Career Life Education 10, 11, 12
- Career Life Connections 10, 11, 12
- English Language Arts 10, 11, 12

Ontario:

- Career Studies Grade 10
- First Nations, Metis and Inuit Studies Grades 9-12
- Business Studies Grades 9-10
- Business Studies Grade 11-12
- English Language Arts Grades 9-10
- English Language Arts Grades 11-12

DURATION

3-4 hours

OVERVIEW

Students will learn from an Indigenous role model of their choice and present their findings to the class. Indigenous role models can be role models in the fields such as health care, education, business, art, activism and more. Enabling students to hear and learn from an Indigenous role model can inspire them to pursue learning opportunities and careers that they may not have considered before. Learning about Indigenous role models also contributes to the spirit of reconciliation by teaching both Indigenous and non-Indigenous students the positive impacts that Indigenous people have on our communities. Students will research a role model that is highlighted in a Fireside Chats video. Students will then create a 3–5 minute multi-media presentation teaching the class about their role model.

MATERIALS

- "Indigenous Role Model Examples" Reproducible
- "Indigenous Role Model Presentation Template"
- "Presentation Checklist"
- Sticky notes and writing instruments (pencils, pens, etc.)
- Computer and internet access

Lesson Plan

☀ ACTIVATE: WHAT MAKES SOMEONE A ROLE MODEL?

To begin this lesson, pose the question: "What makes someone a role model?" Have students turn to a partner and take turns answering the question. As students are discussing, provide each pair with a sticky note to write their ideas on. When they are ready to share, students will place their sticky note on the board. The teacher will then read out all the answers to the class.

Next, pose the question: "Who are some of your role models"? Again, have students turn to their partners and share their answers. Provide a second sticky note. Pairs will write their answers and place their sticky note on the board. The teacher will read out all the answers.

Once teachers have read out the answers, discuss the concept of "representation" with the class. Representation in this context refers to *the inclusion, active participation, and portrayal of people in various sections of society*. Ask how many role models they named are People of Colour. How many of those are Indigenous? Answers will vary.

Inform the class that for too long Indigenous people have been represented in the media either using harmful stereotypes or not at all. However, today, that is changing, and Indigenous people are represented more positively in media and in all facets of society. Inform the class that today they will have the opportunity to learn about an Indigenous role model using Future Pathways Fireside Chat Videos.

ACQUIRE: FUTURE PATHWAYS FIRESIDE CHATS VIDEOS

Choose a Fireside Chats video to show the class as a whole-class example.

Examples:

  - Activism/Education: Christine M'Lot, Teacher
  - Arts/Graphic Arts: Monique Aura Bedard, Art Maker
  - Athletes/Sports and Recreation: Richard Pellissier-Lush, Collegiate Athlete
  - Business and Entrepreneurship: Jessica Dumas, Life Coach
  - Community Development: Diane Roussin, Non-Profit Project Director
  - Computer Science: Dallas Wapash-Flett, Video Game Designer
  - Culture: Curtis Clearsky, Food Relations Coordinator
  - Elected Officials: Senator Yvonne Boyer, Senator
  - Entertainment: Dakota Bear, Hip-Hop Artist and Activist
  - Health and Science: Taylar Belanger, Traditional Herbalist
  - Skilled Trades: Raven Beardy, Pilot

Debrief the video by asking the class the following questions:

  1. Where is this role model from?
  2. What type of education does this role model have?
  3. What does this role model do as a job or career?
  4. What was a source of inspiration for this role model?
  5. What interesting fact did you learn about this role model?
  6. Does this role model have some of the qualities you wrote about with your partner? Which ones?

Next, using the "Indigenous Role Model Examples" reproducible, share a few examples of Indigenous role models' students may want to learn from and research further.

Finally, encourage students to use their own devices to explore the Fireside Chat website at https://www.firesidechats.ca

Students will choose a role model they want to learn more about. Students may have to watch a few videos or read a few stories before they decide who they want to present on.

APPLY: INDIGENOUS ROLE MODEL PRESENTATION

Once students have selected a role model they want to present on, review the "Presentation Checklist" together as a class so students know how they will be graded.

Inform students that they will create their own 3–5-minute presentation on their chosen role model. Students may choose the style of presentation such as a poster or a PowerPoint presentation.

Students will research the following key points:

  1. Early Life
  2. Educational Journey
  3. Career/Job Description

4. Their Inspiration/Goals/Aspirations
5. Interesting Facts and Advice
6. How They Fit the Definition of a Role Model

ASSESSMENT

The activating activity is a form of formative assessment. Teachers will be able to check students' prior knowledge on the subject and correct misconceptions as they read out the students' answers from the sticky notes.

The presentation project is a form of summative assessment. Using the checklist provided, teachers are encouraged to mark students' presentations and provide them with constructive feedback. Students can use this feedback to improve future presentations.

The discussion questions are a form of self-assessment. Check for students' new understanding about role models and representation.

INDIGENOUS ROLE MODEL PRESENTATION TEMPLATE

Use the template below to help with your research for the presentation.

Student Name: _____

Fireside Chat Role Model: _____

Early Life
What does the role model say about their home, childhood, and upbringing?

_____

_____

_____

_____

Educational Journey
What was this role model's educational journey like?

_____

_____

_____

_____

Career/Job Description
Describe the role model's past jobs. What do they currently do now?

_____

_____

_____

_____

Inspiration/Goals/Aspirations
What is their source of inspiration? What goals does this role model have for the future? What other aspirations do they have?

_____

_____

_____

_____

Interesting Facts and Advice

What interesting facts did you learn throughout this interview? What advice does the role model give youth?

_____

_____

_____

_____

How They Fit the Definition of a Role Model

How does this person fit your definition of a role model? What qualities of a role model do they possess?

_____

_____

_____

_____

INDIGENOUS ROLE MODEL PRESENTATION CHECKLIST

Student Name:

0 NO	1 SOME- WHAT	2 YES	
			Presentation included an overview of the role model's early life
			Presentation included an overview of the role model's educational journey
			Presentation included a description of the role model's jobs – past and present.
			Presentation included an overview of the role model's sources of inspiration, goals, and aspirations
			Presentation clearly described how this person fits the definition of a role model, including the qualities they possess.
			The presentation was engaging, and the presenter spoke with appropriate volume.
			The presentation was well-organized, easy to follow and was in the 3–5-minute time frame.

Teacher Feedback:

INDIGENOUS ROLE MODEL EXAMPLES

This is a non-exhaustive list of Indigenous role models working in various job sectors.

Elected Officials/Politics Sector:
Chief: Christopher Derickson
Senator: Yvonne Boyer
Member of Parliament: Mumilaaq Qaqqaq
Lawyer: Alyson Bear

Culture Sector:
Vegetable Farmer: Joy Hall
Food Relations Coordinator: Curtis Clearsky
Friendship Centre Administrator: Carly Chartier
Weaver: Todd DeVries
Traditional Herbalist: Tayler Belanger

Arts/Graphic Sector:
Multimedia Artist: KC Hall
Art Program Coordinator: Kevin Wesaquate
Designer: Ovila Mailhot
Graphic Designer: Alexandra Jarett

Activism Sector:
Action Therapist: Caitlin Richard
Youth Mentor: Caid Jones
Program Coordinator: Amber Crittenden
Kairos Blanket Exercise Facilitator: Theland Kicknosway

Skilled Trades Sector:
Electrician: Sateana Goupil
Hair Stylist: Krista Paul
Pilot: Raven Beardy
Engineer: James Harper

Education Sector:
Indigenous Educator: Christine M'Lot
University Professor: Dr. Dara Kelly
Language Teacher: Dwayne Drescher
Life Skills Coach: Jojo Tootoosis

Business & Entrepreneurship Sector:
Social Entrepreneurship: Nicole Taylor Sterritt
Life Coach: Jessica Dumas
Business Founder: Jared Kozak
Entrepreneur: Inuujaq Leslie Fredlund
Vice President of Indigenous Financial Services: Jon Davey

Entertainment Sector:
Actor/Actress: Anna Lambe
Writer: Jacquie Black
Singer/Songwriter: Evan Redsky
Hip-Hop Artist: Dakota Bear
Musician: Theresa Warbus
Model: Joleen Mitton
Social Media Influencer: Michelle Chubb

Community Development/Youth Engagement Sector:
Community Outreach Worker: Larissa States
Domestic Violence Court Case Worker: Kayla Maurice
Outreach Coordinator: Linnea Dick
Project Director: Diane Roussin
Law Student: Marley Dunkers
Social Worker: Alyssa Carpenter
Child and Family Services Worker: Linsay Willier

Health and Science Sector:
Surgeon: Donna May Kimmaliardjuk
Doula: Pihêsiw Crane
Nurse: Shania Petit
Medical Doctor: Kali Romano
Social Worker: Chelsea Kelly

Computer Science Sector:
Game Designer: Dallas Flett
Software Engineer: Ashlee Foureyes

Athletes/Sports and Recreation Sector:
Hockey Player: James Lappin
Program Coordinator: Carson Roche

Lesson One: Dallas Storm Flett-Wapash

Activity: Design a Video Game Concept

CURRICULUM CONNECTIONS	Alberta, Northwest Territories and Nunavut:

- Aboriginal Studies Grades 10-12
- English Language Arts Grades 10-12
- English Language Arts Grades 10, 11, 12: Uqausiliriniq Strand.
- Information and Communication Technology Grades 10-12

British Columbia and Yukon:

- Contemporary Indigenous Studies Grade 12
- Computer Studies Grade 10
- English Language Arts Composition Grades 10, 11, 12
- Media Design Grade 10, 11, 12
- Web Development Grade 10
- Digital Communications Grade 11

Ontario:

- First Nations, Metis, and Inuit Studies Grades 9-12
- English Language Arts Grades 9-10
- English Language Arts Grades 11-12
- Introduction to Computer Science Grades 10-11
- Introduction to Computer Programming Grade 11
- Computer Programming Grade 12
- Computer Science Grade 12

DURATION	4-5 Hours

OVERVIEW	In this lesson, students will explore the topics of Indigenous representation in digital media and video games, video game design, and interactive media design. Students will participate in a sticky-note activity where they will get to express their own favourite video games. Teachers will then debrief the activity with questions relating to Indigenous representation in the students' favourite games, and what elements the students may think go into designing such games. Students will watch Dallas Storm Flett-Wapash's interview with Fireside Chats. Students will complete a three-part project based on creating a video game concept. Students will write a paragraph of what their video game would be like, including concept art and a 3D model of one of their video game characters. Students will be assessed by a "Paragraph Writing" rubric, and an artwork self-assessment.

MATERIALS	

- Computer Access for each student
- Sticky notes (enough for each student)
- White paper
- Drawing and colouring materials (pencils, pencil crayons, fine-tip markers, etc)
- Air-dry clay, modelling clay or plasticine of many different colours
- Cardboard or paper plates
- Access to a digital media application (optional)
- "Create Your Own Video Game Concept Project" handout
- "Paragraph Writing Rubric" handout
- "Concept Art and 3D Model Self-Assessment Rubrics" handout

ACTIVATE: YOUR FAVOURITE VIDEO GAME

To begin the lesson, instruct the students that today we will be exploring Dallas Storm Flett-Wapash's career journey as a videogame designer. To begin, hand out one sticky note to each student. On the sticky note, students will write a list of their favourite video games. Give students 1-2 minutes to write down their answers. When they are done, encourage them to come to the board and stick it on.

Once everyone's answers are on the board. Start sharing some of the answers with the class. If keen, the teacher can keep a tally for the video games most represented to see which is the class's favourite video game.

To debrief the activity ask the following question:
1. Do any of these video games have Indigenous representation?
2. Would you like to become a videogame designer?
3. What kind of elements do you think go into making a video game?

ACQUIRE: DALLAS STORM FLETT-WAPASH'S FIRESIDE CHAT

https://www.firesidechats.ca/video/dallas-storm-flett-wapash

Dallas Flett-Wapash is a Saulteaux First Nations man from Keeseekoose First Nation in Kamsack, Saskatchewan. Currently, Dallas resides in Brandon, Manitoba. Dallas is a video game designer and an interactive media artist. Dallas was motivated to create video games due to the good experience he had with them as a kid. As he grew up, Dallas noticed the lack of Indigenous representation in mainstream video games. That motivated him more to become a videogame designer. He wanted to use his ambition to fill in the gaps of Indigenous voices in video game design.

Start the video of Dallas Storm Flett-Wapash's interview with Fireside Chats. Alternatively, students can read his story in the textbook or on the web site. In the interview, Dallas discusses his career and education journey as a video game and interactive media designer. Dallas focuses on the lack of Indigenous representation in the videogame field, and how that motivated him to become a designer.

To debrief the video, ask the class the following questions:

1. What motivated Dallas to become a videogame designer?
2. What was the biggest obstacle that Dallas faced on his career journey to become a videogame designer and interactive media artist?
3. What is one piece of advice Dallas would give his younger self?

Students will use the learning from Dallas Storm Flett-Wapash's interview to understand what goes into creating a videogame and implement it into their own concept design.

APPLY: CREATE A VIDEO GAME CONCEPT

Students will use the learning from Dallas' interview and become video game designers themselves! Students will create their own video game concept. There will be three parts to this project. Students will describe their video games in writing (who, what, when, where, why), draw one concept art for the video game, and create a 3D model of one of their video game characters.

The written piece will follow a paragraph rubric and include the what, the who, then when, the where, and the why of the video game. The why part will explain the video games purpose. Is the video game supposed to teach players a lesson or skill? Is the video game just for pleasure and fun?

The concept art will show scenes directly from the video game they are imagining. Students will follow a checklist to create their concept art. Students will be provided white paper, drawing and colouring materials to create their art. Students will need to create concept art for their video games. The concept art could show the various characters, a scene from the video games, the landscape of where the game takes place, etc.

The 3D model will represent either the main character or main villain in the student's video game concept. Students will be provided with either air-dry clay, modelling clay, or plasticine to create their models. Provide students with a piece of cardboard or a paper plate to create their models on. Instruct students to write their first name, and section if applicable, on the top of the paper plate. Students will self-assess themselves with how well they believe they create their models. Students will give themselves a mark for their 3D models. It is up to the teacher's discretion if the marks are changed. Teachers will provide feedback and a final mark for the entire project.

ASSESS:

The sticky notes activity is a form of formative assessment. This activity will enable teachers to assess group learning and student communication skills.

The debriefing questions after Dallas' interview with Fireside Chats is a form of formative assessment. Teachers will be able to check what students took away from Raven's video and make connections to the other parts of the lesson.

The Create a Video Game Concept project is a summative assessment. Students will be assessed by a paragraph rubric, and an artwork self-assessment. Students will give their models a mark. Teachers will provide students with feedback and a total mark for the project. It is at the teachers discretion if they keep the original mark the students have chosen for their models. Teachers will check if the three parts of the project flow well together, check for creativity and individuality, and provide students with feedback of how well they completed the project, improvements they could make in the future, and any other comments they may have,

PART ONE: WRITTEN PIECE

Write an 8-10 (you may include more if needed) sentence paragraph describing your video game concept. Include the who, what, when, where and why. *Use the space below to create your draft*. Please neatly handwrite or type your final copy to hand into the teacher.

_____

_____

_____

_____

_____

_____

_____

_____

_____

_____

_____

_____

_____

_____

_____

_____

_____

_____

_____

_____

_____

_____

PART TWO: CONCEPT ART

Either using white paper, or a digital application such as Paint, Photoshop, or Procreate, create a piece of concept art for your video game. You have creative control over your concept art. You must follow the checklist below of what to include. You may draw out all your characters, a scene from your video game, the landscape it takes place on etc.

Concept Art Checklist:

- Include an element from my video game that is described in my written piece.
- Use of different colours, textures, and designs in my art.
- Creativity and uniqueness
- Neatness and quality of design
- Use of a lot of time and consideration into my art piece.

PART THREE: D MODEL OF A CHARACTER

Either using white paper, or a digital application such as procreate or an avatar creator, you will create a 3D model representation of your main character or main villain. You have creative freedom over your character. Choose their height, weight, facial features, hairstyle, clothing choices, etc. When video game designers are making video games, they need to make 3D models of every character in the game. Even characters that you don't get to play!

3D Model Checklist:

- My character has a face, body, and clothing (if applicable)
- Use of different colours, textures, and designs in my art.
- Creativity and uniqueness
- Neatness and quality of model design
- Use of a lot of time and consideration into my model.

PARAGRAPH WRITING ASSESSMENT RUBRIC:

Student Name: _____

CATEGORIES OF PERFORMANCE:	BEGINNER (0)	BASIC (1)	INTERMEDIATE (2)	ADVANCED (3)
Opening sentence	The sentence is incomplete and does not state the main idea.	The sentence is complete, but does not state the main idea.	The sentence is complete and adequately states the main idea.	The sentence is complete and clearly states the main idea.
Supporting sentences	Some sentences are incomplete or run-on and do not support the main idea.	Some sentences are incomplete or run-on, but support the main idea.	Most sentences are complete and support the main idea.	All sentences are complete and support the main idea.
Closing sentence	The sentence is incomplete and does not sum up the paragraph.	The sentence is complete, but does not sum up the paragraph.	The sentence is complete and adequately sums up the paragraph.	The sentence is complete and clearly sums up the paragraph.
Organization of ideas	Ideas in the reflection are disorganized and do not support the main idea, causing a confusion of meaning.	A few ideas in the reflection do not support the main idea or are out of place, causing a confusion of meaning.	Ideas in the reflection support the main idea, but could be organized more clearly.	Ideas flow in the reflection and clearly support the main idea, creating meaning.
Spelling, capitalization, and punctuation	There are many errors in spelling, capitalization, and punctuation.	There are some errors in spelling, capitalization, and punctuation.	There are only a few errors in spelling, capitalization, and punctuation.	There are no errors in spelling, capitalization, or punctuation

/15

Teacher Feedback:

Final Mark:

_____/15 + _____/24 = _____/39

CONCEPT ART AND 3D MODEL SELF-ASSESSMENT:

Give yourself a mark for each category by either adding a checkmark or highlighting the box.

CONCEPT ART SELF-ASSESSMENT RUBRIC

CATEGORIES OF PERFORMANCE:	NEEDS IMPROVEMENT (1)	GOOD (2)	GREAT (3)	OUTSTANDING (4)
Time and Effort	Class time was not used wisely, and there was no additional effort.	Class time was not always used wisely, but I did do some additional work at home.	Class time was used wisely. I could have put in more time and effort at home.	Much time and effort went into the planning and design. I put in a lot of work at home as well as at school.
Creativity and Uniqueness	The project lacked creativity, individuality, and concepts may be from a different video game.	The project could have used more creativity or uniqueness. I used a few colours.	Project was very creative. I used different colours and designs.	Project was exceedingly creative. I used a variety of colours and designs. I thought outside of the box!
Quality and Neatness of Design	Scenes are unclear and disorganized	Scenes show the setting	Scenes show a detailed setting including landscape, buildings, journeys etc.	Scenes show a detailed setting including landscape, buildings, journeys, plus demonstrate mood of the game (cheerful, frightening, surreal etc.)

/12

3D MODEL SELF-ASSESSMENT RUBRIC

CATEGORIES OF PERFORMANCE:	NEEDS IMPROVEMENT (1)	GOOD (2)	GREAT (3)	OUTSTANDING (4)
Time and Effort	Class time was not used wisely, and there was no additional effort.	Class time was not always used wisely, but I did do some additional work at home.	Class time was used wisely. I could have put in more time and effort at home.	Much time and effort went into the planning and design. I put in a lot of work at home as well as at school.
Creativity and Uniqueness	The project lacked creativity,individuality, and concepts may be from a different video game.	The project could have used more creativity or uniqueness. I used a few colours.	Project was very creative. I used different colours and designs.	Project was exceedingly creative. I used a variety of colours and designs. I thought outside of the box!
Quality and Neatness of Design	There were little or no facial features, My character was disorganized or confusing	My character design was a bit confusing or disorganized. I could have put more thought into it.	My character is unique, has facial features, has hair, and clothing.	My character design went above and beyond. It looks like a real character straight from a video game.

/12

Total /24

Lesson Two: Ashlee Foureyes

Activity: EarSketch Coding

CURRICULUM CONNECTIONS	**Alberta, Northwest Territories and Nunavut:** • Aboriginal Studies Grades 10-12 • Information and Communication Technology Grades 10-12 **British Columbia and Yukon:** • Contemporary Indigenous Studies Grade 12 • Computer Programming Grade 11-12 • Computer Studies Grade 10 • Media Design Grade 10, 11, 12 • Web Development Grade 10 • Digital Communications Grade 11 **Ontario:** • First Nations, Metis, and Inuit Studies Grades 9-12 • Introduction to Computer Science Grades 10-11 • Introduction to Computer Programming Grade 11 • Computer Programming Grade 12 • Computer Science Grade 12
DURATION	2 hours
OVERVIEW	Note: We strongly suggest you familiarize yourself with the online coding program EarSketch before you begin this lesson. EarSketch is a free coding platform that teaches students core topics of computer science, music, and music technology. There are many lessons that the website offers In this lesson, students will explore the topics of software development, coding, Indigenous women in STEM, and software engineering. Students will participate in a KWLQ Medicine Wheel activity on the topic of software development and coding. The Medicine Wheel graphic organizer helps to depict that all learning - what we already know, what we want to know, what we have learned, and what we will learn in the future - is all connected and a continuous cycle. Students will watch Ashlee Foureyes' interview with Fireside Chats. Students will then use EarSketch to code a song! To save time and/or space, students may work individually or as a pair. Students will be assessed using a "Coding Song Project Rubric".
MATERIALS	• Computer Access for each student • KWLQ Medicine Wheel handout for each student • EarSketch - https://earsketch.gatech.edu/landing/#/learn • Resource - EarSketch Music Tutorial Guide: https://www.teachers.earsketch.org/earsketch-tutorials • "Coding Song Project Rubric"

Lesson Plan

✳ ACTIVATE: KWLQ MEDICINE WHEEL

To begin the lesson, instruct the students that today we will be looking at the education and career journey of Ashlee Foureyes, an Indigenous software development engineer.

Hand out the KWLQ Medicine Wheel graphic organizer to each student. They will fill out half of the sheet now, and half after watching Ashlee's interview with Fireside Chats. Pose the question "*What is software development and what is coding?*". Instruct students that they will be filling out the wheel about software development and coding. In the Eastern Doorway quadrant (the right-hand side), students will fill out the K or the "Know". Instruct students to fill in anything they might know about software development and/or coding. Next, in the Southern Doorway quadrant (the bottom), students will fill in the W or the "Want to learn?". Students will write in information they want to learn about software development and/or coding.

After watching Ashlee Foureye's interview with Fireside Chats, or reading her story in the text-book or online, students will fill in the last two quadrants - Learned and Questions.

ACQUIRE: ASHLEE FOUREYES' FIRESIDE CHAT

http://firesidechats.ca/video/ashlee-foureyes

Ashlee Foureyes is an Indigenous woman from Maskwacis in the Wetaskiwin area in Alberta. Ashlee is a software development engineer for Amazon. Ashlee grew up in a small rural community with limited access to technology. Ashlee started her education journey with the idea that she would become an accountant since she had a love for mathematics. However, Ashlee took a coding elective class once and found her passion. Since then she turned her education journey onto computer sciences and started her career journey as a software development engineer.

Start the video of Ashlee Foureyes' interview with Fireside Chats. In the interview, Ashlee discusses her career and education journey as a software engineer at Amazon. Ashlee has been on an exciting career journey and found her passion by accident.

Instruct students to keep their KWLQ Medicine Wheel graphic organizers in front of them. As they watch Ashlee Foureyes video, encourage students to fill out the Learned section of their sheets. In the Learned section, students will write new information they did not know about software engineering, coding, or even about the education and career journey to do such things. In the Questions section, students should write at least 5 questions they still have about software engineering and/or coding.

To debrief the video, ask the class the following questions:

1. What is some advice Ashlee has for young people looking into post-secondary?
2. Why is adaptability Important?
3. How has the Covid-19 pandemic impacted the way we use technology and computers?

Students will apply the foundational learning from the KWLQ activity, and Ashlee's interview with fireside chats to try some coding of their own!

APPLY: EARSKETCH CODING

We strongly suggest you familiarize yourself with EarSketch before you begin this lesson.

In this activity, students will learn the basics of coding with EarSketch and build foundational coding information. Students will compose a short song through code using either the programming language Python or Javascript. EarSketch is a free web-based coding platform that teaches students core topics of coding, computer science, music, and music technology. There are many lessons that the website offers.

To start, go to the EarSketch website - https://www.teachers.earsketch.org/ and ensure you click "Hour of Coding" under the "TEACH" tab. On this tab, it'll take students through how to use EarSketch.

Students will create their own song by coding. The teacher, or the student, will pick the programming language that they will use. The options are Python or Javascript. Have each student start at the same time; so all students get the same amount of time. Instruct students to try to be creative and use their time wisely. Hand out the Coding Song Rubric to each student so they know how they will be assessed.

First students will go through a tutorial. In the tutorial they will first be shown the code editor. Here they will be able to explore their workspace to compose music. The code editor is a text editor with numbered lines. Next, students will be shown the run button. By clicking this button, the codes that the students create will turn into music.

Students will then be shown where they can preview their music. The Digital Audio Workstation (DAW) is a visual timeline of the code. Students will then be able to play their code by pressing the play button on top. Beside the play button, is the rewind and the loop button.

On the left-hand side of the screen, students will be able to explore code and music samples in the browser area. There are three parts to the browser section. Sounds, Scripts and API. In Sounds, students will be able to find thousands of sound collections that they can use. The Scripts section is where their code is automatically saved to. Scripts can include many other pieces by different owners and are sorted by program languages and date. The API section contains audio files that students can also use. After the tutorial, have students create an account so their information and work will not be lost.

Once students go through the tutorial, and create their accounts, they will be able to start coding a song. Encourage students to have fun and refer to their rubric if they have questions about how this will be assessed.

ASSESS:

The KWLQ Medicine Wheel activity is a form of formative assessment. This activity will enable teachers to assess individual learning and growth, and correct any misconceptions students may have about coding and computer science.

The debriefing questions after Ashlee's interview with Fireside Chats is a form of formative assessment. Teachers will be able to check what students took away from Raven's video and make connections to the other parts of the lesson.

The EarSketch Coding activity is a form of summative assessment. Students will be assessed by a Coding Rubric and teacher feedback. Teachers will be able to provide feedback on individual learning and growth with coding, software development and using EarSketch.

TAKE STUDENT LEARNING FURTHER

Activity: EarSketch Computer Science Principles

For students and classes that are very keen on coding, computer science and using EarSketch, there are many lessons and programs that EarSketch offers. The Computer Science Principles module teaches students coding. The eight to ten-week modular curriculum is designed for use within a high school introductory computing course. The curriculum is divided into three units, which are supported by teacher materials. Such as lesson plans, PowerPoint slides, assessments and worksheets in programming languages: Python and JavaScript. This project would take 8-10 weeks to complete.

https://www.teachers.earsketch.org/computer-science-principles

KWLQ MEDICINE WHEEL GRAPHIC ORGANIZER

Use the space below to fill in what you know, what you want to know, what you have learned, and any questions you may still have. Start in the Eastern Doorway (right-hand side) and move clockwise around.

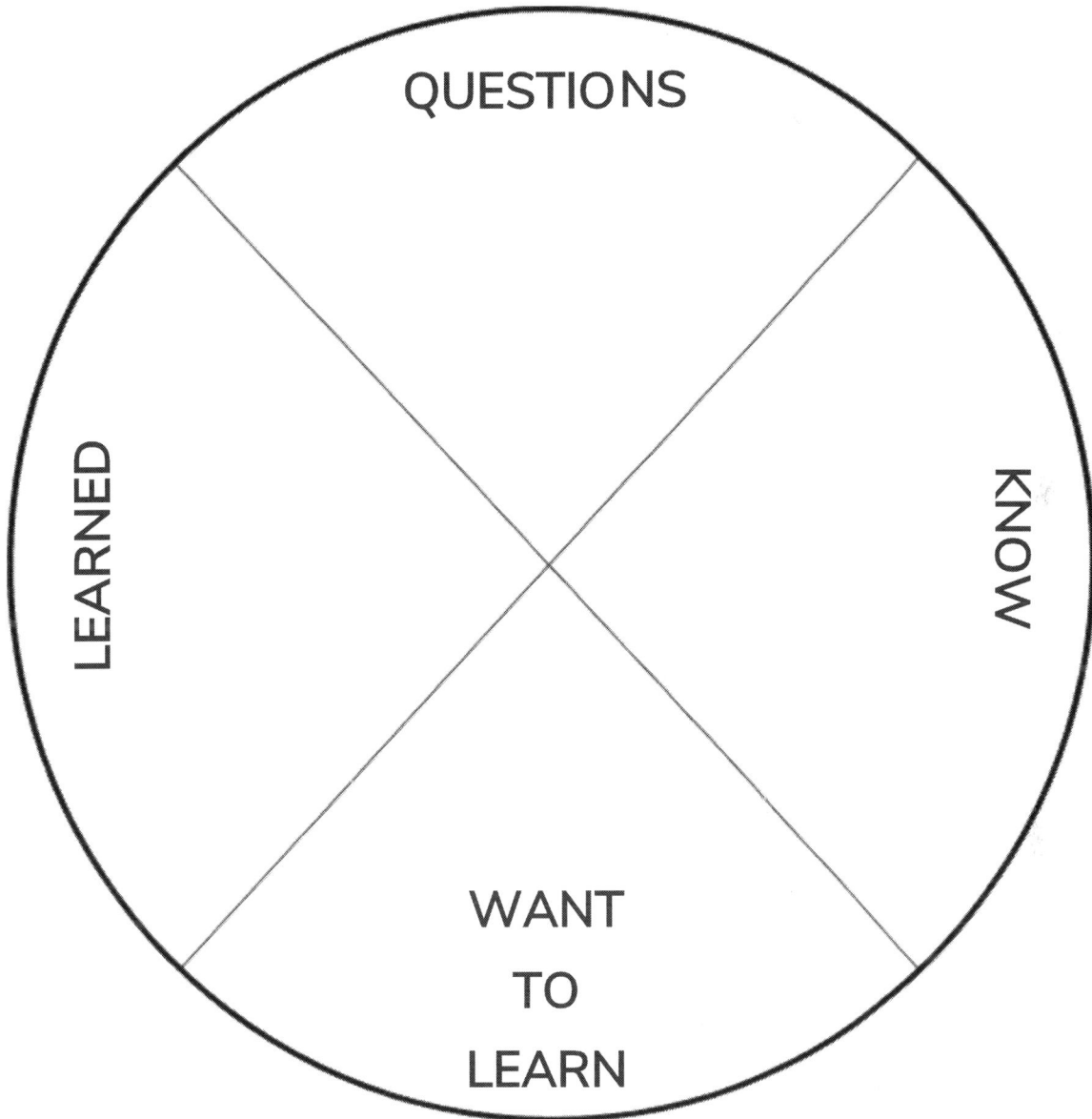

QUESTIONS

LEARNED

KNOW

WANT
TO
LEARN

CODING SONG ASSESSMENT RUBRIC

Name: _____

CATEGORIES OF PERFORMANCE:	BEGINNER (0)	BASIC (1)	INTERMEDIATE (2)	ADVANCED (3)
Tempo and Flow	There is no clear flow or rhythmic pattern to the music.	Music does not have a clear rhythmic pattern and does not flow that easily well.	Music flows somewhat well together, and shows a good rhythmic pattern to the words.	Music flows well together and shows that there is a great rhythmic pattern to the beats.
Composition	There is no contrast, repetition (hook), or transitions between the sections of music.	There is little contrast, repetition (hook) of beats and transitions between sections of music.	Contrast, repetition (hook) of beats and transitions between sections of music is present but, could have been more memorable	The music is catchy, has a recognizable "hook", and transitions well between different sections of the song.
Time, Effort and Creativity	Writing assignments show that no time or effort was put in. Lacks creativity.	Minimal time and effort were used for creativity for the writing assignment.	Some effort and time were used for the assignment.. Lyrics are creative.	Student went above and beyond with the creativity in their lyrics. Shows great time and effort.

/12

Teacher Feedback:

Lesson One: Joy Hall

Activity: "Where is Our Food From?" Inquiry Project

Alberta, Northwest Territories & Nunavut:
- Aboriginal Studies Grades 10-12
- Science Grades 11-12
- Social Studies Grades 10-12
- World Geography Grade 12

British Columbia and Yukon:
- Explorations in Social Studies Grade 11
- Contemporary Indigenous Studies Grade 12
- Life Sciences Grade 11
- Earth Sciences Grade 11
- Science for Citizens Grade 11
- Environmental Science Grade 12

Ontario:
- First Nations, Metis, and Inuit Studies Grades 9-12
- Science Grades 9-10
- Environmental Science Grade 11
- Science Grade 12, University/College Preparation
- World Cultures, Grade 12, University/College Preparation

DURATION

2-3 hours

OVERVIEW

Throughout this lesson, students will learn about Indigenous farming/agriculture, growing traditional medicine plants, and the various traditional medicines and foods that can be found in their own backyards. Students will connect the four aspects of life (Mother Earth, Plants, Humans and Animals) including impacts and connections to gardens and agriculture.

Students will experience how growing their own food, and having food sovereignty in their own backyards, helps connect them to the land. Students will watch Joy Hall's interview about her career as an organic vegetable farmer. Students will take the information learned in the video and apply the concepts to their own province. Students will perform an inquiry-based research project about what types of native fruits and vegetables that can be cultivated, eaten and grown in their province and where their favourite foods come from.

Students will create a brochure highlighting their research. Students will be assessed from an inquiry-project brochure rubric. To take students learning further, students may create a classroom garden.

MATERIALS

- Loose leaf paper
- Writing instruments for students (pens, pencils, etc.)
- Computers and internet access
- Medicine Wheel Graphic Organizer (optional)
- "Where is our food from?" Brochure Inquiry Project
- "Where is our food from?" Brochure Inquiry Project Rubric
- Where is our Food From? Inquiry-Project Brochure Teacher Feedback Form

ACTIVATE: ASPECTS OF LIFE AND THE GARDEN MEDICINE WHEEL ACTIVITY

In this activating strategy students will learn about how the four aspects of life connect or impact the garden and our food systems. *The four aspects of life are: Mother Earth, Plants, Animals, and Humans. Plants include all vegetation including flowers, trees, moss and lichens. Mother Earth includes the elements of air, earth, water, and fire. Air includes wind and weather change. Earth includes soil, mud and rock.*

To begin the lesson, ask students to take out a piece of loose leaf paper. You will draw a Medicine Wheel on the board. Draw a large circle on the board and divide it into four quadrants with an X. This will be the model for students for their Medicine Wheel graphic organizers. Label on the outside of the top quadrant with an "N" or "North"; the right-side quadrant with an "E" or "East"; The bottom quadrant with an "S" or "South"; and the left-side quadrant with a "W" or "West". Instruct students to do the same on their papers. Alternatively, instead of students drawing their own Medicine Wheels, you may hand out a Medicine Wheel Graphic Organizer that is attached below.

In the top quadrant (or Northern Doorway, as it is called in the Medicine Wheel) write inside at the top "Mother Earth". In the East quadrant, write "Plants"; In the South quadrant write "Animals"; and in the West quadrant write "Humans". Instruct students to do the same on their papers.

When using a Medicine Wheel graphic organizer, you will always start in the East. So for this activity, you will start with "Plants". Instruct students that farming and gardening is a food system. We get food from gardens. Talk about the four aspects of life and connect them to the garden. The four aspects of life are Plants, Animals, Humans and Mother Earth. Pose the question: "How do plants connect to gardens?". Let students have a moment to think to themselves. Have students raise their hands to give some answers. Write their answers down in the Plants section of the Medicine Wheel. Instruct students to write down the answers too. Try to have at least 3-5 examples for each quadrant. Post the same question for each quadrant.

- How do animals connect to or impact gardens?
- How do humans connect to or impact gardens?
- How does Mother Earth connect to or impact gardens?

Potential Answers:
Plants:
- Plants grow in a garden
- Trees give shade to a garden
- Weeds can be invasive in a garden
- Vegetables make up a garden
- Seeds germinate in a garden

Animals:
- Rabbits eat vegetables in the garden
- Earthworms help the soil of the garden
- Birds could eat the seeds
- Some insects need gardens to thrive and eat the leaves
- Small burrowing animals may call the gardens soil home

Humans:
- Humans plant gardens
- Humans eat from gardens
- Humans play in some gardens such as corn fields (corn maze)
- Humans can pollute gardens
- Humans may work in a garden

Mother Earth:

- Gardens need rain to survive
- Wind may damage crops
- Forest fires could damage crops
- Plants need soil to grow from
- If the weather is too cold for too long, it may shorten the growing season or the ability to grow

After finishing the Medicine Wheels, instruct students that you will now be learning about Joy Hall, an organic vegetable farmer!

ACQUIRE: JOY HALL'S FIRESIDE CHAT VIDEO

Joy Hall is a mother, entrepreneur, organic vegetable farmer, and the owner of Joy Farms. Joy is from the Hall family from Sq'ewqéyl (Skowkale) First Nation, British Columbia and the Felix family from Sts'ailes (Chehalis) First Nation, British Columbia. Joy Farms uses organic farming techniques. Joy started to learn about making traditional medicines and how to grow her own plants and foods. Which then led to Joy attending the Tsawwassen Farm School at Kwantlen Polytechnic University. Joy Farms provides healthy organic foods and veggie boxes for her community members. Joy also educates about healthy food and nutrition as well as issues related to unhealthy eating habits , while connecting everything she does back to the Land and culture.

Start the video of Joy Hall's interview with Fireside Chats. In the video, Joy Hall talks about her job as an organic vegetable farmer, and her passion for nutrition and health. After showing the video, ask the students if they have any questions or misconceptions about Joy's interview.

To debrief the video, ask the class the following questions:

1. How did Joy become an organic vegetable farmer?
2. What are some diseases that Joy has researched that can be improved by eating a healthy, organic diet?
3. Do you know what kinds of food are locally grown where we live?

In Joy's interview, she talks about how it is important to know where your food comes from. Inform students that individually, they will be completing an inquiry-based project researching what food is grown in their province, and where some of their favourite food is grown elsewhere in the world.

APPLY: WHERE IS OUR FOOD FROM? BROCHURE INQUIRY PROJECT.

Students will be performing an inquiry-based research project on two major questions and creating a brochure displaying their research. Students will be researching what foods are grown readily in their own province, and then they will discover where three of their favourite foods are grown.

Questions:

What types of food grow in my own province?

     a. State what province you live in.
     b. What type of fruit are grown? (Find 5 examples)
       a. Where are they grown?
       b. How are they grown?
     c. What type of vegetables are grown? (Find 5 examples)
       a. Where are they grown?
       b. How are they grown?

Where are the foods I am eating coming from, if they are not from my province?

a. List *three* foods you like to eat that do not grow in your province.
Example: Mangos, Avocadoes, Bananas
b. Where do these foods grow?
c. How are these foods grown

What other questions do you have?
a. List **three** other questions you have. Questions can be about the environmental impact of farming, sustainable farming practices, the history of farming in your area, traditional Indigenous farming methods, traditional Indigenous diets, etc...

Students will create a brochure showcasing their information. This brochure is for students to show that this information is important for others to see. This project will help students connect to where their food is coming from, and bring awareness to any issues that they may discover about food systems when they are researching how different fruits and vegetables are grown.

ASSESS:

The Aspects of Life Medicine Wheel activity is an example of formative assessment. Teachers will be able to check students' prior knowledge about how humans, animals, plants, and Earth impact gardens while correcting any misconceptions students may have as they share their answers.

The inquiry-based research project is a form of summative assessment. Students will be given a mark based on the inquiry-project research guidelines (40 marks) and the brochure organization rubric (20 marks) provided below. Students will be marked out of a total of 60 marks.

With the teacher's feedback form, check for students' new understanding and correct any misconceptions students may have. Give the students feedback on their project. Teachers are encouraged to give feedback on how well students conducted their research, how well organized their project was, or tips for future research projects.

TAKE STUDENT LEARNING FURTHER

Activity: Classroom Garden
If students show a keen interest in learning more about agriculture, gardening or where and how food grows, as a class you can grow your own classroom garden! To make a classroom garden, there will need to be a lot of planning. Planning should start in the winter (January/February). You will need to plan:

- Your overall vision for the classroom garden
- Where and what you're going to plant
- Resources in your community
  - Are there places that may be able to donate seeds, soil, garden boxes, gardening tools, etc.?
- The roles everyone will have while creating the garden
- A budget (if applicable)

There are many resources online that have guides on starting an outdoor classroom garden! This is a fun project with many cross-curricular applications.

MEDICINE WHEEL GRAPHIC ORGANIZER

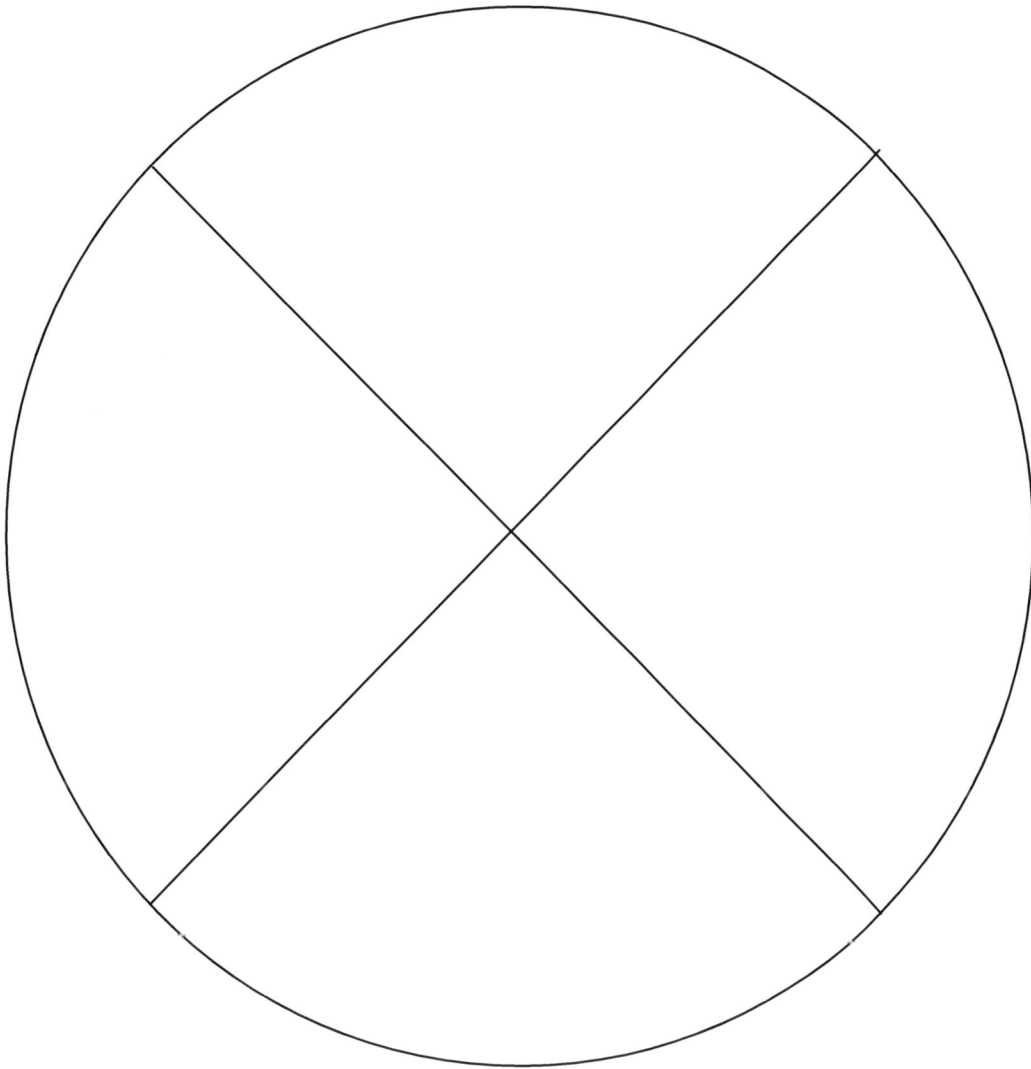

INTRODUCTION:

For this project, you will be making a brochure highlighting the research you conduct on where our food comes from. You will research where three fruits and three vegetables are grown in your own province, and research where three other foods are grown in the world. You will then research three of your own questions.

Information to be Included:
- Front Page/Cover (1 mark)
  - Create a Title
  - Image/Photo
  - Your name, date, class
- What types of food grow in my own province?
  - State what province you live in.
  - Find **five** examples of different **fruits** that are grown in your province.
    - » Where are the fruits grown? (5 marks)
    - » How are the fruits grown? (5 marks)
  - Find **five** examples of different **vegetables** that are grown in your province.
    - » Where are the vegetables grown? (5 marks)
    - » How are the vegetables grown? (5 marks)
- Where are the foods I am eating coming from, if they are not from my province?
  - List **three** foods you like to eat that do not grow in your province. Example: Mangos, Avocadoes, Bananas (3 marks)
  - Where do these three foods grow? (3 marks)
  - How are these foods grown? (3 marks)
- What other questions do you have?
  - List **three** other questions that you have (Questions can be about the environmental impact of farming, sustainable farming practices, the history of farming in your area, traditional Indigenous farming methods, traditional Indigenous diets, etc...)
  - Answer your three questions (10 marks)

Marking Scheme:
40 marks – Information in the brochure (see information to be included above)

20 marks – The brochure organization and design (see Marking Rubric below)

= 60 marks

WHERE IS OUR FOOD FROM? INQUIRY-PROJECT BROCHURE ORGANIZATION AND DESIGN RUBRIC

STUDENT NAME:

	4	3	2	1	0
Organization of Information Presented	Each section in the brochure is clear, all information is presented	75% or more sections of the brochure are clear and/or information is presented.	60% or more sections of the brochure are clear and/or information is presented.	50% or more sections of the brochure are clear and/or information is presented.	The sections of the brochure are not clear and/or no information is presented.
Content Accuracy and Information Validity	All facts in the brochure are accurate and match cited resources.	80-99% of the facts in the brochure are accurate	60-79% of the facts in the brochure are accurate.	50-60%of the facts in the brochure are accurate.	Less than 50% of the facts in the brochure are accurate.
Attractiveness and Design	The brochure Has exceptionally attractive formatting and well-organized information.	The brochure has attractive formatting and well-organized information.	The brochure has well organized information or format but not both.	The brochure has slightly organized information or format but not both.	The brochure's formatting and organization of material is confusing to the reader.
Graphics/ Photos	Graphics match the topic and text in sections where placed. Each section has no more than two graphics and there are at least a total of three graphics used.	Graphics go well with the text, but there are so many (more than two per section)that they distract from the text.	Graphics go well with the text, but there are too few (less than three graphics for the entire brochure) and the brochure seems "text-heavy".	Graphics do not go with the accompanying text or appear to be randomly chosen.	No graphics or photos are presented.
Spelling and Mechanics	No spelling errors and all sections of the brochure are free of writing errors.	No more than 2 spelling and/or writing errors are present.	No more than 5 spelling and/or writing errors are present.	No more than 10 spelling and/or writing errors are present.	More than 10 spelling and/or writing errors are present.
			Total Marks:		/20

WHERE IS OUR FOOD FROM? INQUIRY-PROJECT BROCHURE

Student Name:

Brochure Information Mark: _____/ 40

Brochure Organization: _____ /20

Final Mark: _____/60

Teacher Feedback:

_____

_____

_____

_____

_____

_____

_____

_____

_____

_____

_____

_____

_____

_____

_____

_____

_____

_____

_____

_____

_____

_____

_____

Lesson Two: Curtis Clearsky

Activity: Classroom Feast

CURRICULUM CONNECTIONS	**Alberta, Northwest Territories & Nunavut:** • Aboriginal Studies Grades 10-12 • Social Studies Grades 10, 11, 12 **British Columbia and Yukon:** • Culinary Arts Grades 10, 11, 12 • Food Studies Grades 10, 11, 12 • Social Studies Grades 10 • Explorations in Social Studies Grade 11 • Contemporary Indigenous Studies Grade 12 **Ontario:** • Social Studies Grades 9-12 • First Nations, Metis, and Inuit Studies Grades 9-12
DURATION	2-3 hours
OVERVIEW	Throughout this lesson, students will explore the ideas of food sovereignty, Indigenous food relations, the importance of food access and security in Canada and how food brings people together. The food sovereignty movement is gaining traction globally. Food sovereignty is the newest and most innovative approach to achieving the end goal of long-term food security for all. Students will watch Curtis Clearsky's interview in which he speaks about his career in Indigenous food relations. Curtis talks about how food is a spiritual experience. After watching the video, students will learn the Anishinaabe Feast Teaching. The Feast is a spiritual experience. Students will learn about the four sacred foods in a feast, the ideation of a spirit dish and ways feasts bring people together. Students will then come together and apply the ideas of food relations, food sovereignty and the feast teachings to create a classroom feast of their own. Students will create a menu based on the four sacred foods, and then actively prepare all the food. Finally, students will participate in a classroom feast self-assessment and peer-assessment where they will analyze their groups roles in creating the feast.
MATERIALS	• Anishinaabe Feast Teachings Teacher Guide • Feast Teachings - Medicine Wheel Graphic Organizer • Bannock Recipe (optional) • Stew Recipe (optional) • Wild Rice Recipe (optional) • Rice Pudding Recipe (optional) • Classroom Feast Self-Assessment • Kitchen access, fridge access, and cooking/eating tools (pans, pots, spoons, forks, plates, measuring cups, aluminum foil/parchment paper, knives, cutting boards, etc.) • Ingredients for cooking (look to each recipe for what ingredients you will use)

Lesson Plan

*Before starting this lesson, research traditional Feast teachings in your local community by speaking with an Elder or Knowledge Keeper. *We recommend inviting an Elder or Knowledge Keeper into your classroom to give this teaching (see "Acquire" section). Then read through the Anishinaabe Feast Teachings Teacher Guide.*

☀ ACTIVATE: WHAT IS "INDIGENOUS FOOD SOVEREIGNTY"

To begin this lesson, you will break down the definition of "Indigenous Food Sovereignty". To start, write the word "Sovereignty" on the board or chart paper. Pose the question *"What does the word 'Sovereignty' mean?"*. Have students think to themselves for about thirty seconds and then discuss with a classmate. Have students share their answers. Write their answers on the board. Share the general definition of Sovereignty with the class. **Sovereignty is supreme power or authority. It is the authority of a state to govern itself or another state.** Have students write down this definition in their notes.

After explaining the definition, write the word FOOD below the word Sovereignty. Connect the two words with an arrow. Pose the question *"What does food sovereignty mean?"* Scaffold with the definition of sovereignty and how this may relate to a person's food and food source. Have students discuss with a classmate. Students can then share their answers. Write some of their answers on the board. After discussing, share the general definition of Food Sovereignty with the class. **Food Sovereignty is the right of peoples to healthy and culturally appropriate food produced through sustainable methods, and the right to define their own food and agriculture systems."** Have students write down this definition in their notes.

Finally, write the word INDIGENOUS below the term Food. Connect the two terms with an arrow. Pose the question "Using the two other definitions, what do you think Indigenous Food Sovereignty is?". Let students have some time to think to themselves and then share their thoughts with a neighbor. Have students share some of their thoughts and write their answers down. After discussing, share the general definition of Indigenous Food Sovereignty with the class. **Indigenous food sovereignty is the indigenous approach to addressing our right to meet our own needs for balanced and traditional Indigenous foods. This is the freedom to choose how much or what kind of food we hunt, fish for, gather, grow, and eat. It is the responsibility to uphold Indigenous relationships with the land, plants and animals that provide us with our food.** Have students write down this definition in their notes.

🧑‍🏫 ACQUIRE: CURTIS CLEARSKY'S FIRESIDE CHAT VIDEO AND FEAST TEACHING

Curtis ClearSky has been working in Indigenous food relations since 2006. Curtis has led the Tu'wusht Project from 2013-2016 at the UBC Farm on beautiful Musqueam territory. With the Tu'wusht Project, Curtis connected intergenerational urban Indigenous people in the Vancouver BC area to culturally connected food growing and preserving. In 2016 Curtis led the research and development of a Social Innovation project that was based on traditional Indigenous food trade economies. Curtis is now involved in the First Nations Food System project supporting over 70 First Nations communities in BC in food security development .

Start the video of Curtis Clearsky's interview with Fireside Chats. In the video, Curtis talks about his career in the Indigenous Food Relations Industry. Encourage students to write down ideas from the video into their notes. After showing the video, ask the students if they have any questions or misconceptions about Curtis' interview. Instruct that in Curtis' interview, he talks about how food brings people together. Inform students that as a class, we will come together with food and have a classroom Feast!

Hand-out the *Feast Teachings - Medicine Wheel Graphic Organizer* Handout. Instruct students that with the information we learned earlier about Indigenous Food Sovereignty and from the ideas and teachings we heard from Curtis Clearsky, you are going to have a classroom Feast based on traditional aspects. Before you have a classroom Feast however, students will need to learn the significance of the feast.

Invite a local Elder or Knowledge Keeper into your class to share teachings around the Feast, or refer to the *Anishinaabe Feast Teachings Teacher Guide*.

If using the *Anishinaabe Feast Teachings Teacher Guide*, instruct students that Feasting is an important cultural celebration that occurs throughout different times in a year (13 Moon cycle) for many different reasons. Feasts occur after ceremonies. Such as at the end of a Pow-wow, to conclude a Naming Ceremony, after a funeral, and more. Feasts also occur during special occasions like birthdays, first thunder of the year, and weddings. Even during holidays. A feast can also occur to give thanks to the Creator, to our ancestors, or even for the community. Like all important cultural practices, feasts begin with an offering of tobacco, and all attendants smudge. Next, before everyone eats a Spirit Dish is made. A Spirit Dish is made to connect us to the Creator and to our ancestors. A Spirit Dish is made up of tiny portions of the food that is being served. Placed on a biodegradable plate or placed upon birch bark. The Spirit Dish is then placed in nature to feed the spirits who work so hard to protect us. Sometimes there are specific practices and protocols during a feast. For example, women usually prepare the feast, and Elders eat first. Traditional foods are served at feasts such as wild rice, corn, berries, bannock, and wild meat/fish.

Draw a large circle on the board and divide it into four quadrants with an X. This will be the model for students for their Medicine Wheel graphic organizers. Label on the outside of the top quadrant with an "N" or "North"; the right-side quadrant with an "E" or "East"; The bottom quadrant with an "S" or "South"; and the left-side quadrant with a "W" or "West". Instruct students to do the same on their papers.

In the top quadrant (or Northern Doorway, as it is called in the Medicine Wheel) write inside at the top "Wild Meat". In the East quadrant, write "Berries"; In the South quadrant write "Corn"; and in the West quadrant write "Wild Rice".

Start in the East. Like the Sun rising, we always start in the East (right-side) when using a Medicine Wheel graphic organizer. Berries are an important part of the feast because they symbolize life. In the Anishinaabe culture, strawberries represent women and blueberries represent men. Eating them together represents the life that men and women create together. We eat berries at the feast to celebrate life.

Next, in the South, we talk about the importance of corn. Corn is important in a feast because it symbolizes Mother Earth, what we receive from Mother Earth and reminds us to respect nature. As we eat the corn, we are to be thankful for all the food we can receive from Mother Earth's soils.

In the West, we talk about the importance of wild rice. Wild rice is important in a feast because it represents water. Wild rice grows in shallow waters and the plant can reach great lengths, up to ten feet. Eating wild rice reminds us of the importance of water for all life. We need to respect water and remember that water is sacred. Without water, we wouldn't exist.

Finally, in the North, we talk about the importance of wild meat/fish. When we eat wild meat/fish we should be thankful towards the animal for sustaining our lives. We need to respect all animals and where they live and grow. Wild meat/fish also represents relationships and sharing. In the circle of life, all living things depend on one another. Such as friends, family, and classmates depend on each other. Making relationships very important. In relationships, we can show love and thanks by sharing. In a feast, the sharing of food is extremely important. As people get together to feast, usually everyone brings something to share with one another.

Underneath the Feasting Medicine Wheel, there will be a few definitions for the students to complete and a self-reflection question.

To debrief the video, ask the class the following questions:

1. How does Curtis describe food sovereignty? Why is connection to food important to Curtis?
2. What kind of experience does food bring Curtis?
3. How did Curtis get into food growing?

APPLY: CLASSROOM FEAST

Next class, students can start planning their classroom feast. You will want to have around four to give groups. It is up to the teacher's discretion what food is made for the feast. You can follow this guide for the dishes and recipes or come up with our own!

Four Groups of foods to prepare:

1. Bannock - See Bannock Recipe
2. Stew Meat and corn (Beef, pork, chicken, wild meat, meat substitute) - See *Stew*
3. Wild Rice and Water - See *Wild Rice Recipe*
4. Fresh Berries (Dessert)

Instruct students they will be working in groups to make each food item. It is at your discretion how you split up the groups. There should be at least 2 people, no more than 4 in each group. If there are more recipes you want to make for your feast, then by all means go for it! This is just a starting off point.

Group One: Bannock

This group will be in charge of making the bannock. To make bannock based on the recipe attached, you will need:

- Flour,
- Sugar,
- Margarine/lard,
- Water/milk,
- Baking powder, and
- Salt.

Instruct students to follow their recipe. They will need to preheat their ovens to 375 degrees. Next they will need to measure out their ingredients and bring it back to their work station. The group should make 2-4 loaves of bannock. The secret to light and fluffy bannock is not to overmix the dough. After adding in all the ingredients and mixing the dough. Students will place the dough on a parchment or aluminum foil and gently flatten out the dough. They will then poke the dough all over with a fork. Then the students will place the bannock in the oven for 20-30 minutes or until golden brown.

Group Two: Stew

This group will be in charge of making a stew. To make stew you will need:

- 2 lbs of Meat (Cubed beef, cubed pork, cubed chicken, or a meat substitute such as black beans)
- 4-5 Carrots cut into bite sized pieces
- 4-5 Stalks of Celery cut into bite sized pieces
- 1 large white onion diced
- 3 cloves of garlic crushed
- 3 potatoes cut into bite sized pieces
- 1 cup of frozen peas
- 1 cup of frozen corn
- 1 large can of tomato sauce
- 4L of broth or water
- Salt, pepper, bay leaf, garlic powder, paprika seasoned to taste
- 2 tbsp of oil

Instruct students to follow their recipe. They will first need to chop up all their vegetables and meat for the stew. Next, they will add the oil and the diced onions and let it cook for 2-3 minutes on medium heat. Then add the cubed meat and cook until done. If you are using a meat substitute like beans, they can be added when you add the carrots. Next they will add the garlic and celery. Cook for 2-3 minutes Then add the carrots. After adding the carrots, season the food to taste. Then add the jar of tomato sauce and broth. Stir. When it starts to boil, add in the potatoes. When the stew comes back to a boil, add the frozen peas and corn. Cook until veggies are tender.

Group Three: Wild Rice and Water

This group will be in charge of making wild rice. Wild rice is relatively easy to make so you may want to make this group the smallest. This group should also be in charge of helping to clean up the kitchen and prepare the cutlery/plates for the feast. To make wild rice you will need:

- 2 cups of wild rice
- 2 minced garlic
- Dash of salt
- Water

Thoroughly rinse the wild rice in a strainer under cold water. Next you will want to bring a large pot of water to boil. Use 6 cups of water per 1 cup of wild rice. Add a dash of salt to the water. When boiling, add the wild rice. Watch the rice carefully. It should take 40-55 minutes to cook. The wild rice is done when the rice is tender. When the rice looks like it is splitting down the middle seam, it is likely done. Students may season it however they want.

This group will also be in charge in ensuring that everyone has water for the feast. They may prepare water cups/bottles before the feast and hand-out the water to people at the feast.

Group Four: Berry Dessert

This group will be in charge of making a dessert for the feast that consists of berries. You may use fresh or frozen berries. Berries that are typically used are strawberries, blueberries, raspberries, blackberries, cherries and saskatoon berries.

There are many different recipes you could make with berries. Cake, muffins, rice pudding, crepes, jams, etc. are all great options. Have group four plan what they want to make and see what ingredients they have. Berries can also just be eaten as is, or with some whipped cream on top.

Example: Rice Pudding and Berries

For this recipe, you will need:

- 3 cups milk
- 1 cup Minute® White Rice
- 1/4 cup sugar
- 1/4 cup raisins (optional)
- 1/4 teaspoon salt
- 2 large eggs
- 1 teaspoon vanilla
- Cinnamon (optional)
- Fresh or frozen berries

To begin, instruct students to measure out all their ingredients. Back at their workstations, they will combine milk, rice, sugar, raisins (optional) and salt in a medium saucepan. They will bring the mixture to a boil, stirring it constantly. Reduce heat to medium-low and simmer the mixture for 6 minutes, stirring it occasionally.

In a small bowl, lightly beat the eggs and vanilla. Stir a small amount of the hot mixture into eggs. This is called tempering. Stir constantly and pour another small amount of the milk mixture into the eggs. After you get about ⅓ of the milk mixture into the eggs, slowly pour the egg mixture right into the pot. Stir it together, constantly, and cook on low heat for about a minute until thickened. Do not boil this mixture. After about a minute remove it from the heat. Let the rice pudding stand 30 minutes on the counter or let it thicken quicker in the fridge. Sprinkle with cinnamon, if desired. Place fresh or frozen berries on top.

After the food is prepared, you may start your Feast. Typically, the Feast is either eaten on the ground/floor together or sitting at their tables. To start, either yourself (the teacher) or a class leader to help prepare the spirit dish. In the spirit dish you will add a very tiny portion of each food that was prepared. This dish will sit in the middle of the attendants until there is a time where you can go to offer it outside. Next, serve the food in whichever way suits your class the best. Whether that be potluck style, have someone prepare each plate, buffet style, etc. Enjoy the time together as a classroom community!

After the Feast, provide students with the Classroom Feast Assessment provided below. Students will mark themselves and their group members with a checklist based on their participation in preparing the feast and answer a self-reflection question.

ASSESS:

The activating strategy of term definitions is a form of formative assessment. Teachers will be able to check students' prior knowledge about food sovereignty and Indigenous food sovereignty and correct any misconceptions students may have as they share their answers.

The Medicine Wheel Graphic Organizer is a form of formative assessment. This is a place for students to record and organize the information gained in the lesson.

Handout the *Classroom Feast Assessment* and have students self-assess and peer-assess their participation, cooperation and attitude.

The reflection questions are a form of summative self-assessment. Check for students' new understanding and correct any last misconceptions students may have. Students will be giving themselves a mark for their participation in preparing the feast.

TAKE STUDENT LEARNING FURTHER

Activity: Food Sovereignty in Canada Research Project
If students show a keen interest in learning more about Indigenous food sovereignty or food sovereignty in general, students can do an inquiry-based learning project on the topic. Students can research food sovereignty on a local, national or global scale.

Students can work individually, in pairs or in groups. Students will guide their own learning by creating their own inquiry questions to research.

Some inquiry-question examples:

- What are the Seven Pillars of Food Sovereignty in Canada?
- How do farmers maintain sustainable practices?
- How does food sovereignty and sustainable food systems in Alberta compare to Yukon?
- How does Canada's food sovereignty for Indigenous peoples compare to Indigenous peoples in the states?

Students will spend time researching their topic based on the questions they have. Finally, students should have the opportunity to analyze their findings through an essay, poster, multimedia presentation or other mode of assessment.

FEAST TEACHINGS MEDICINE WHEEL

NAME:

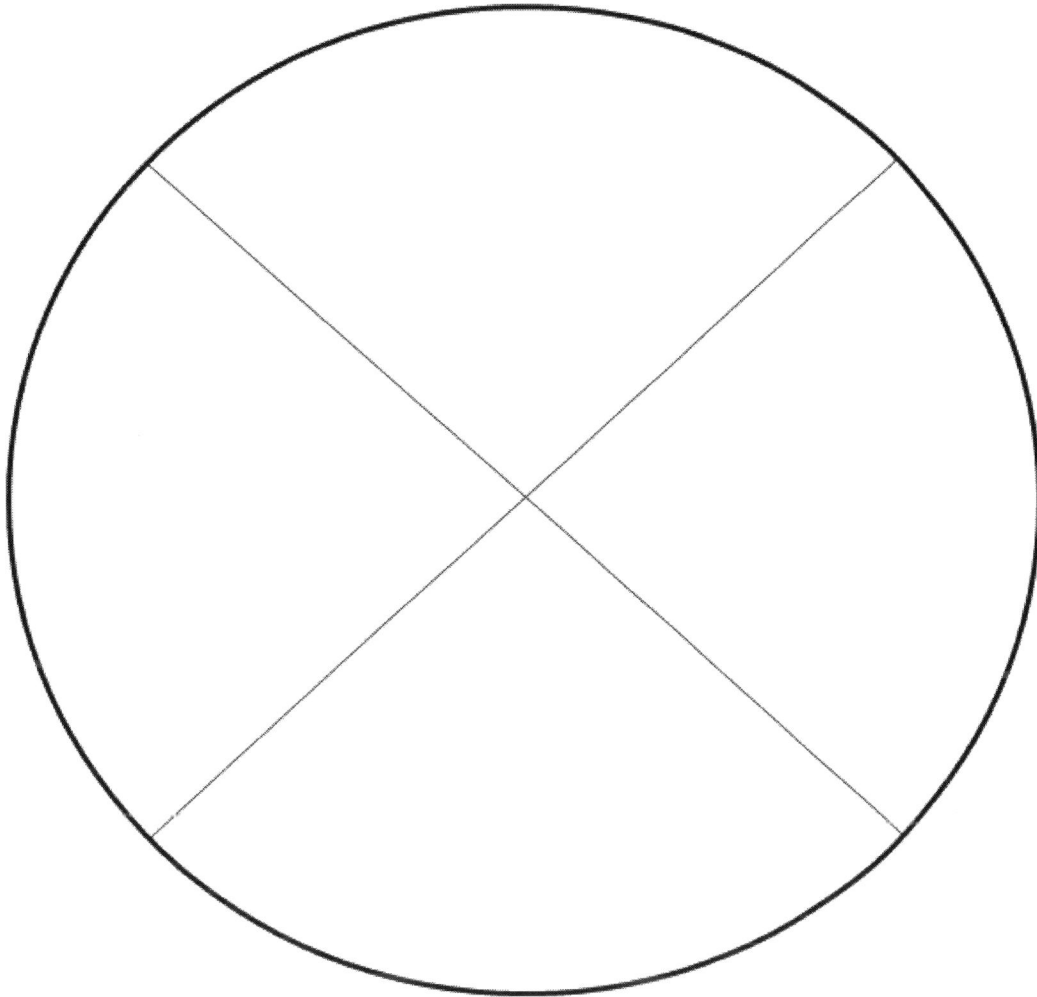

Spirit Dish:

_____

_____

_____

What is an important feast/holiday you do with your family/friends? Why is it important?

_____

_____

_____

Feasting is an important cultural celebration that occurs throughout different times in a year (13 Moon cycle) for many different reasons. Feasts occur after ceremonies. Such as at the end of a Pow-wow, to conclude a Naming Ceremony, after a funeral, and more. Feasts also occur during special occasions like birthdays, first thunder of the year, and weddings. Even during holidays. A feast can also occur to give thanks to the Creator, to our ancestors, or even for the community. Like all important cultural practices, feasts begin with an offering of tobacco, and all attendants smudge. Next, before everyone eats a Spirit Dish is made. A Spirit Dish is made to connect us to the Creator and to our ancestors. A Spirit Dish is made up of tiny portions of the food that is being served. Placed on a biodegradable plate or placed upon birch bark. The Spirit Dish is then placed in nature to feed the spirits who work so hard to protect us. Sometimes there are specific practices and protocols during a feast. For example, women usually prepare the feast, and Elders eat first. Traditional foods are served at feasts such as wild rice, corn, berries, bannock, and wild meat/fish.

The Medicine Wheel is made up of four quadrants. The top quadrant is called the Northern Door-way. It is usually labelled on the outside with an "N" or as North. The right-side quadrant is called the Eastern Doorway. It is usually labelled on the outside with an "E" or as East. The bottom quadrant is called the Southern Doorway. It is usually labeled with an "S" or as South. Finally, the left-side quadrant is called the Western Doorway. It is usually labelled with a "W" or as West.

The North quadrant of the Medicine Wheel will be labelled Wild Meat. The East quadrant will be labeled Berries. The South quadrant will be labelled Corn and in the West quadrant label it Wild Rice.

Start in the East. Like the Sun rising, we always start in the East (right-side) when using a Medicine Wheel graphic organizer. Berries are an important part of the feast because they symbolize life. In the Anishinaabe culture, strawberries represent women and blueberries represent men. Eating them together represents the life that men and women create together. We eat berries at the feast to celebrate life.

Next, in the South, we talk about the importance of corn. Corn is important in a feast because it symbolizes Mother Earth, what we receive from Mother Earth and reminds us to respect nature. As we eat the corn, we are to be thankful for all the food we can receive from Mother Earth's soils.

In the West, we talk about the importance of wild rice. Wild rice is important in a feast because it represents water. Wild rice grows in shallow waters and the plant can reach great lengths, up to ten feet. Eating wild rice reminds us of the importance of water for all life. We need to respect water and remember that water is sacred. Without water, there would be no us.

Finally, in the North, we talk about the importance of wild meat/fish. When we eat wild meat/fish we should be thankful towards the animal for sustaining our lives. We need to respect all animals and where they live and grow. Wild meat/fish also represents relationships and sharing. In the circle of life, all living things depend on one another. Such as friends, family, and class-mates depend on each other. Making relationships very important. In relationships, we can show love and thanks by sharing. In a feast, the sharing of food is extremely important. As people get together to feast, usually everyone brings something to share with one another.

Example of Completed Feast Medicine Wheel:

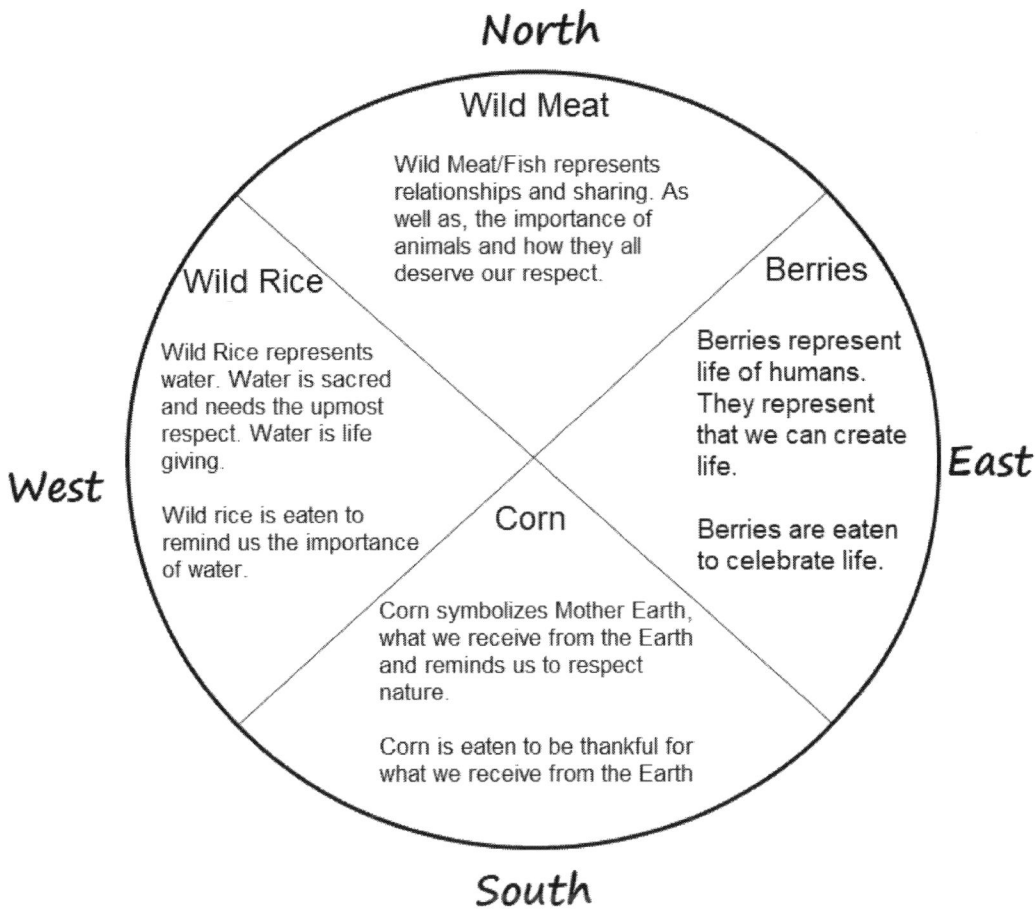

North

Wild Meat

Wild Meat/Fish represents relationships and sharing. As well as, the importance of animals and how they all deserve our respect.

Wild Rice

Wild Rice represents water. Water is sacred and needs the upmost respect. Water is life giving.

Wild rice is eaten to remind us the importance of water.

West

Corn

Corn symbolizes Mother Earth, what we receive from the Earth and reminds us to respect nature.

Corn is eaten to be thankful for what we receive from the Earth

Berries

Berries represent life of humans. They represent that we can create life.

Berries are eaten to celebrate life.

East

South

Spirit Dish:

A Spirit Dish is made to connect us to the Creator and to our ancestors. A Spirit Dish is made up of tiny portions of the food that is being served. Placed on a biodegradable plate or placed upon birch bark.

What is an important feast/holiday you do with your family/friends? Why is it important?

Students may write about different holidays or occasions that occur in their lives that include a feast, such as birthdays, weddings, Christmas, Ramadan, Hanukkah, Winter Solstice, etc. They need to explain why it is important to them and to their family.

BANNOCK RECIPE:

The order in which the ingredients are listed are how it is added to make the bannock. You will need:

- 3c flour
- 3 heaping tbsp margarine
- 2 ½ tsp baking powder
- 2 tbsp white sugar
- Pinch of salt
- 1c of milk or water

1. Preheat the oven to 375 degrees.

2. Take 3 cups of flour and place into a large mixing bowl. Add 3 heaping tbsp of margarine to the flour. Mix with a fork or pastry blender until the flour looks crumbly. Like small pebbles.

3. Add 2 ½ tsp of baking powder to the mixture. Mix together.

4. Next, Add 2 tbsp of sugar and a pinch of salt. Mix together.

5. Slowly add one cup of milk/water and mix. Add more water if it has too much flour but, only add a little at a time. The secret to soft bannock is to not over mix.

6. Once the dough comes together it will look shaggy. Gently flatten out the dough on a flat pan and poke with a fork all over.

7. Bake in the oven for 20-30 minutes or until golden brown.

STEW RECIPE

To make stew you will need:

- 2 lbs of Meat (Cubed beef, cubed pork, cubed chicken, or a meat substitute such as black beans)
- 4-5 Carrots cut into bite sized pieces
- 4-5 Stalks of Celery cut into bite sized pieces
- 1 large white onion diced
- 3 cloves of garlic crushed
- 3 potatoes cut into bite sized pieces
- 1 cup of frozen peas
- 1 cup of frozen corn
- 1 large can of tomato sauce
- 4L of broth or water
- Salt, pepper, bay leaf, garlic powder, paprika seasoned to taste
- 2 tbsp of oil

1. First need to chop up all the vegetables (onion, garlic, carrots, celery, potatoes) and meat for the stew. Use different cutting boards and knives for the vegetables and for the meat.

2. Place 2 tbsp of oil into a large pot and turn the heat up to medium. Add the diced onions and let it cook for 2-3 minutes.

3. Next, add the cubed meat and cook until meat is completely done. If you are using a meat substitute like beans, they can be added when you add the carrots.

4. Next add the garlic and celery. Cook for 2-3 minutes

5. Then add the carrots and season the food to taste with salt, pepper, garlic powder, paprika, etc.

6. Add the jar of tomato sauce and broth. Stir.

7. When it starts to boil, add in the potatoes

8. When the stew comes back to a boil, add the frozen peas and corn.

9. Cook until veggies are tender. Taste stew and season more if needed.

WILD RICE RECIPE

TakingITGlobal INSPIRE INFORM INVOLVE Lesson Two: Curtis Clearsky

To make wild rice you will need:

- 2 cups of wild rice
- 2 minced garlic
- Dash of salt
- 12 cups of Water

1. Thoroughly rinse the wild rice in a strainer under cold water.

2. Next you will want to bring a large pot of water to boil.

3. Use 6 cups of water per 1 cup of wild rice. Use one pot for every 6 cups.

4. Add a dash of salt to the water.

5. When boiling, add the wild rice. Watch the rice carefully. It should take 40-55 minutes to cook. The wild rice is done when the rice is tender. When the rice looks like it is splitting down the middle seam, it is likely done.

6. Season however you want, with garlic, salt, fresh parsley, etc.

RICE PUDDING WITH BERRIES

For this recipe, you will need:

- 3 cups milk
- 1 cup Minute® White Rice
- 1/4 cup sugar (white or brown)
- 1/4 cup raisins (optional)
- 1/4 teaspoon salt
- 2 large eggs
- 1 teaspoon vanilla
- Cinnamon (optional)
- Fresh or frozen berries

1. To begin, measure out all your ingredients.

2. Combine 3 cups of milk, 1 cup of rice, ¼ cup of sugar, raisins (optional) and ¼ tsp of salt into a medium saucepan.

3. Bring the mixture to a boil, stirring it constantly.

4. Reduce heat to medium-low and simmer the mixture for 6 minutes, stirring it occasionally.

5. In a small bowl, lightly beat the eggs and vanilla. Stir a small amount of the hot mixture into eggs. This is called tempering.

6. Stir constantly and pour another small amount of the milk mixture into the eggs. After you get about ⅓ of the milk mixture into the eggs, slowly pour the egg mixture right into the pot.

7. Stir it together, constantly, and cook on low heat for about a minute until thickened. Do not boil this mixture. After about a minute remove it from the heat.

8. Let the rice pudding stand 30 minutes on the counter or let it thicken quicker in the fridge.

9. Sprinkle with cinnamon, if desired.

10. Place fresh or frozen berries on top.

	EXCELLENT	GOOD	SATISFACTORY	NEEDS IMPROVE-MENT / MISSING
Clear Opinion	Author states a clear opinion and issues a call to action through arguments based on evidence.	Author states an opinion and issues a call to action through arguments based on evidence.	Author states an opinion using evidence	Author is missing a clear opinion and/or evidence
Use of Evidence	Author uses compelling evidence to support the opinion and cites reliable sources.	Author uses strong evidence to support the opinion, using reliable sources	Author uses some evidence to support the opinion	Author does not use evidence to support the opinion
Analysis and Persuasion	Editorial convincingly argues point of view by providing relevant background information, using valid examples, acknowledging counterclaims, and developing claims -- all in a clear and organized fashion.	Editorial argues point of view by providing relevant background information, using valid examples, acknowledging counter-claims -- all in a clear and organized fashion.	Editorial attempts to providing relevant background information but is missing one of the following: using valid examples, acknowledging counterclaims; developing claims; all in a clear and organized fashion.	Editorial is missing 2 or more of the following: Providing relevant background information; using valid examples; acknowledging counterclaims; developing claims; clear and concise language
Grammar and Mechanics	The editorial is error-free	Minor errors found in grammar, capitalization or punctuation	Major error found in grammar, capitalization or punctuation	Many errors throughout that interfere with meaning

SELF-REFLECTION

Answer the following questions below in full sentences. If you run out of room, use a separate piece of paper.

How do you think having a Feast relates to food relations and community? *(4 marks)*

_____

_____

_____

_____

_____

_____

_____

_____

In many First Nations communities, food is scarce and food sovereignty is non-existent. How would having a Feast like we did today be different if food was plentiful and nations had food sovereignty? Similar? *(4 marks)*

_____

_____

_____

_____

_____

_____

_____

_____

What was something new or interesting you have learned from watching Curtis Clearsky's interview? Participating in the classroom Feast? *(4 marks)*

_____

_____

_____

_____

_____

_____

_____

Lesson Three: Carly Chartier

Activity: My Support System

CURRICULUM CONNECTIONS	**Alberta, Northwest Territories and Nunavut:** • Aboriginal Studies Grades 10-12 • English Language Arts Grades 10-12 • English Language Arts Grades 10, 11, 12: Uqausiliriniq Strand **British Columbia and Yukon:** • Contemporary Indigenous Studies Grade 12 • English Language Arts Composition Grade 10 • English Language Arts Composition Grade 11 • English Language Arts Composition Grade 12 • English Language Arts First Peoples Grade 12 • Physical and Health Education Grade 10 **Ontario:** • English Language Arts Grades 9-10 • English Language Arts Grades 11-12 • First Nations, Métis, and Inuit Studies Grades 9-12 • Health and Physical Education Grades 9-12 • Personal Life Management Grade 12 • Dynamics of Human Relationships Grade 11 • Exploring Family Studies Grades 9-10
DURATION	1-2 hours
OVERVIEW	Throughout this lesson, students will participate in a Sharing Circle where they will create a sense of community among each other to enhance their relationships with their peers. The purpose of the Sharing Circle used as part of classroom instruction is to create a safe environment in which students can share their point of view with others. Students will then watch Carly Chartier's interview about her career working at the Selkirk Friendship Centre where she works in Human Resources helping community members find resources/supports and information about post-secondary opportunities. Students will take the information learned in the video and apply the concepts to their own lives by creating a visual of the support systems they have in their own lives. Students will self-assess their final projects based on the rubric posted below.
MATERIALS	• Grandfather Rock/Talking Stick • Writing instruments for students (pens, pencils, etc.) • Large poster paper or chart paper • Pencil crayons, markers, permanent markers • "Sharing Circle Teacher Resource" (optional) • "Support Systems Visual Activity" Hand Out • "Support Systems Visual Self-Assessment" Rubric

Lesson Plan

*Before starting this lesson, research Sharing Circle/Talking Circle teachings in your local community by speaking with an Elder or Knowledge Keeper; alternatively, read through the Sharing Circle Teacher Guide.

We recommend inviting an Elder or Knowledge Keeper into your classroom to give this teaching (see "Activate" section).

✳ ACTIVATE: SHARING CIRCLE

Invite a local Elder or Knowledge Keeper into your class to share teachings around Sharing Circles/Talking Circles, or refer to the *Sharing Circle Teacher Resource which shares Anishinaabe and Red River Métis teachings.*

In this activating strategy, as a class, you will be participating in a Sharing Circle together. Using Indigenous pedagogies and perspectives creates a culturally responsive classroom; which leads to student empowerment, community spirit, boosts in student self-esteem, increases academic improvement and creates a positive learning environment.

Instruct the class to either move their chairs to form a circle or clear a space for everyone to sit on the floor in a circle. The circle symbolizes completeness, interconnectedness and shows that everyone participating is an equal. Participants in a Sharing Circle are all sitting together; either all on the floor or all on chairs (unless there are special accommodations of why someone can't sit in that fashion, such as a student who has a broken leg, and may not be able to get up from the ground).

If a talking stick, grandfather rock or a feather is unavailable, an everyday object such as a pencil can be used as a talking object. The object is usually passed in a clockwise direction unless taught otherwise by a local Elder or Knowledge Keeper.

Only one person speaks at a time. Only the person holding the talking object may speak. Dialogues are not part of the circle as they can become confrontational. What is said stays within the Circle. This shows respect and builds trust for each other.

There will be two rounds of the Sharing Circle. For the first round each student will introduce themself. They may just say their first name. If a student has a Spirit Name, they can share it at this point in time too. The teacher will introduce themselves first.

For the second round, ask students the question "Who, or what, is an important support in your life?". The teacher will answer the question first in order to model what is expected from the students.

Students will take turns passing around the talking object. Whomever has the talking object is The Speaker. The Speaker may speak for as long as they need to, with respect for the time of others. Silence is an acceptable response to the question. *If a student does not feel comfortable sharing, "I pass" is an acceptable answer. Speaking in a Sharing Circle is voluntary.* Everyone without the talking object are The Listeners. The Listeners will listen with respect and give support to the speaker. What is said in the circle stays in the circle - never repeat anything that is said within the circle, unless you have the permission of the speaker.

As the talking object goes around, the teacher will listen to the students' answers about what, or who, they believe is a major support in their life. There may be many various answers. If you want to further the question, you could ask the students "Why are they a major support to you?"

Examples of possible answers:

- Their parents
- Their teacher
- Their best friend
- The school
- The community centre

After the talking object goes around for the second time, the teacher will close the Sharing Circle with a quick grounding exercise. Teachers may use grounding exercises they already use in their classroom or do some deep breathing. The point of grounding the students is to get their minds ready to continue with the lesson.

After concluding the Sharing Circle, instruct students that you will now be learning about Carly Chartier, an administrative human resource worker for the Selkirk Friendship Centre!

ACQUIRE: CARLY CHARTIER'S FIRESIDE CHAT VIDEO

Carly Chartier is a 29-year-old Métis and Non-Status Youth located in Selkirk Manitoba. Carly is a graduate of Red River College where she studied Human Resource Management and graduated with honours. Carly is employed in her field of studies at The Selkirk Friendship Centre (a non-profit Indigenous organization) in Administration Human Resources providing resources to her community. Carly is also a former community impact partner with the #RisingYouth program at TakingITGlobal.

Start the video of Carly Chartier's interview with Fireside Chats. In the video, Carly Chartier talks about her job working at the Selkirk Friendship Centre where she works in Human Resources helping community members find resources/supports, and information about post-secondary opportunities. Carly works supporting youth in learning and knowing their worth in the workplace. This includes labour laws, financial literacy, and human rights. After showing the video, ask the students if they have any questions or misconceptions about Carly's interview.

To debrief the video, ask the class the following questions:

1. Why should youth think about the emotional and physical parts of their future careers?
2. What one piece of advice does Carly have for youth for their future?
3. What is a support system? What are some examples of people or programs that could be a part of your support system?

In Carly's interview, she talks about how important it is to have a support system in place. Inform students that individually, they will be creating a visual of their own support systems they have in their lives.

APPLY: SUPPORT SYSTEMS ACTIVITY

Students will individually create a visual representation of their support system - either a poster or multimedia presentation.

Instruct students that when talking about a support system they will want to go beyond just a list of reliable people they have in their lives. The students will sort people and organizations by where they see them (e.g., community, home, school), the type of relationship they have with them, and the kind of help they can provide. Students benefit from knowing who, and what, is in their support system. It is important for youth to know when to access the supports they have, and how to access them. It is a powerful skill for a student to know that when they are in need, there is a support system they know how to access independently. Students will complete the Support Systems Visual Activity and then make a visual out of the information on the template. On the template, students will list out their different support systems, write what they think the relationship is like, and what kind of help this support provides.

Using the template, students will then create a visual representation of the people/organizations/resources that are a part of their support system. Students are free to be as creative as they want. Students can create a poster or a multimedia visual.

ASSESS:

The Sharing Circle is a form of formative assessment. Teachers will be able to check students' prior knowledge about support systems and correct any misconceptions students may have about the topic as students share their answers in the Sharing Circle.

The debriefing questions after Carly's interview with Fireside Chats is a form of formative assessment. Teachers will be able to check what students took away from Carly's video and make connections to the other parts of the lesson.

The Support Systems activity is a summative assessment. Students will be given a mark based on the self-assessment rubric where students will reflect on how much content they included, how well their connections go in-depth, and their experience creating their support system visually. Students will be given a final mark out of 25 - 15 marks for their visual support system project and 10 marks for their self reflection questions.

TAKE STUDENT LEARNING FURTHER

Activity: Community Resources Infographic

If students show a keen interest in learning more about resources that are available to them in the community, they can do a research project about what resources are currently available in their community for youth. Students will answer the question "Where can you go in your community to find support and resources for your next big transition in life?" With their research, students will create an infographic. The infographic will give others an idea where they can find different community resources and support. Students can share their infographic broadly, so new community members can find safe spaces to turn to when in need.

Before starting this lesson, research Sharing Circle/Talking Circle teachings in your local community by speaking with an Elder or Knowledge Keeper. We recommend inviting an Elder or Knowledge Keeper into your classroom to give this teaching.

The Sharing Circle Teacher Resource was produced by Marika Schalla after careful considerations as well as input and teachings from other community members and Elders. The Sharing Circle teachings offered in this resource are based on Anishinaabe (Ojibwe) and Red River Métis teachings.

BACKGROUND INFORMATION:

A Sharing Circle may be called different names and used for different reasons - The Talking Circle, The Teaching Circle, The Healing Circle. They all have the same premise and that is the Circle is structured to create a sense of safety and respect. The focus of the Circle is to connect people through communication. In the Circle, people verbalize their knowledge and emotions. It is through listening and sharing that we learn how to get in touch with our true selves and others around us. By creating the form of a circle, people are connected equally in spirit, emotion, mental, and the physical.

The purpose of the Sharing Circle, used as part of classroom instruction, is to create a safe environment in which students can share their point of view with others. In a Sharing Circle, each person is equal, and each person belongs. Participants in a Sharing Circle learn to listen and respect the views of others. Using Indigenous pedagogies and perspectives creates a culturally responsive classroom, which leads to student empowerment, community spirit, boosts in student self-esteem, increased academic improvement and creates a positive learning environment.

Sharing Circle Implementation in Classrooms Guidelines:
1. Participants sit in a circle. The circle symbolizes interconnectedness.
2. Participants are all sitting together either all on the floor or all on chairs (unless special accommodations are needed. Everyone needs to be comfortable).
3. **The Speaker** is the person who is in possession of the talking object. The Speaker is the only one who speaks at that time. Cross dialogue is not part of the Circle as it can become confrontational. Everyone will get a fair chance to be The Speaker.
4. **The Listeners** are the rest of the participants. The Listeners listen with respect and non-judgement. Actively listening, with the heart, allows us to hear the true intent beneath what the speaker is saying. Listen in the way you expect others to hear you.
5. An object such as a grandfather rock or a talking stick is used to show who the Speaker is. The object is passed to the East, in a clockwise direction, unless taught otherwise by a local Elder or Knowledge Keeper.
   - If a talking stick, grandfather rock or a feather is unavailable, an everyday object such as a pencil can be used as a talking object.
6. Introduce yourself. It is polite to introduce yourself in the first round. Your name is very important, as important as you are to the Circle. You may just say your first given name. You can also say your Spirit Name if applicable.
7. In other rounds of the Sharing Circle, silence is an acceptable response to any questions posed in the Circle. Participation as the Speaker in the Circle is completely voluntary. There must be no negative reactions to the phrase, "I pass."
8. Speak from the heart - The Speaker should address the circle from the heart and may speak for as long as they need to, with respect for the time of others.
9. What is said in the circle stays in the circle - never repeat anything that is said within the circle, unless you have the permission of the speaker.

Tips to Remember:
- **Confidentiality** - Who speaks and what is said stays within the Circle. This shows respect and builds trust between us.
- **Non-Judgement** - We are all considered equal in the eyes of the Creator. We try to be

open and honest about ourselves and not hurt others with our words.

- **Keeping the Circle** - Participants make a commitment to attend and remain until the Circle is completed. Once the Circle has begun, no one disrupts the Circle by getting up and leaving. Unless there are extenuating reasons. It is up to the facilitator's (teacher's) discretion.
- **No interruptions** - We respect each other by being silent when someone is sharing. We are actively listening.

SUPPORT SYSTEM VISUAL ACTIVITY

Introduction:

In this activity, you will be creating a visual representation of your support system. You will first use the My Support Systems part to figure out who and what your support system consists of. You will list out who is in your support system, then describe the relationship and the connection you have with this support. The relationship is who they are to you. The connection what kind of help this support provides you.

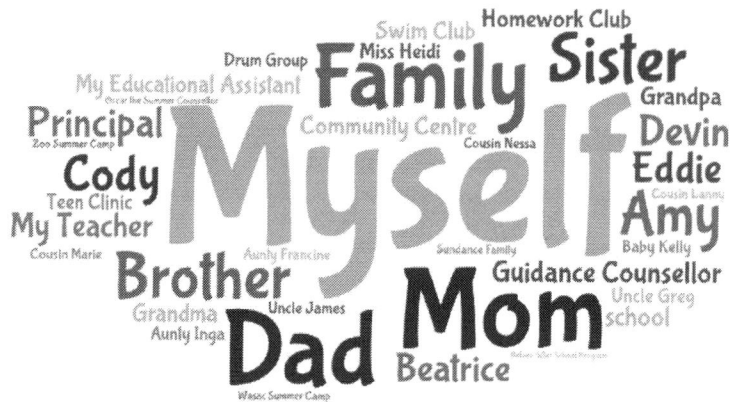

Next, you will use this information to create a visual representation of your support system! This could be done as a poster or as a multimedia presentation. When you are done, you will self-assess yourself with the rubric provided on the back page. Use this rubric as a guide to your visual. When you are finished, give yourself a mark and answer the two reflection questions.

My Support Systems:

Use the three tables to list out who and what is in your support system. List 5-8 supports for each category. Then write out the relationship you have with this support. Last, you will write the connection to the support. The connection is what they provide you with.

EXAMPLE:		
Ms. Schalla	She is my teacher	Ms Schalla provides me with emotional support, teaches me new things, and uplifts me. I can go to her if I have any issues in class.
Ruby Lou	We have been best friends since we were kids.	They provide me with advice, emotional support, and are always there when I need someone. They are always a phone call away.

Home Supports: This includes your family, friends, online friends, and pets.

HOME SUPPORTS	RELATIONSHIP	CONNECTION

School Supports: This includes any school staff, school programs, extra-curriculars, before/after school programs, etc.

SCHOOL SUPPORTS	RELATIONSHIP	CONNECTION

Community Supports: This includes any school staff, school programs, extra-curriculars, before/after school programs, etc.

COMMUNITY SUPPORTS	RELATIONSHIP	CONNECTION

SUPPORT SYSTEM VISUAL ACTIVITY SELF-ASSESSMENT

Use the rubric below as guidelines on how to construct your Support System Visual. Before you hand in your project, give yourself a mark using this rubric and answer the two reflection questions below.

	EXCELLENT (3)	GOOD (2)	NEEDS IMPROVEMENT (1)	MISSING (0)
Inclusion of Support Systems	I showcased 15-24 different supports in my visual project, as well as additional information.	I showcased 15-24 different supports in my visual project but no additional information	I showcased 7-14 different supports in my visual project.	I showcased less than 7 different supports in my visual project.
Organization	The project isexceptionally organized in terms of design, layout, and neatness.	The project is organized in terms of design, layout, and neatness.	The project is slightly disorganized. The project is distractingly messy **OR** poorly designed.	The project is very disorganized. The project is distractingly messy **AND** poorly designed
Creativity	Project was exceedingly creative. I used different colours, images and words. I thought outside of the box!	Project was very creative. I used different colours, images and words.	The project could have used more creativity or uniqueness. I used a few images and colours.	The project lacked images, colour, and words.
Time and Effort	Much time and effort went into the planning and design. I put in a lot of work at home as well as at school.	Class time was used wisely. I could have put in more time and effort at home.	Class time was not always used wisely, but I did do some additional work at home.	Class time was not used wisely, and there was no additional effort.
Mechanics	No grammatical, spelling or punctuation errors.	Almost no (1-3) grammatical, spelling or punctuation errors	A few (4-6) grammatical, spelling, or punctuation errors.	Many (7+) grammatical, spelling, or punctuation errors
Self-assess and give yourself a mark out of 15.			/15	

REFLECTION QUESTIONS

Answer the following questions on a separate piece of paper. Staple to the back of this paper.

What issues did you come across during this project? Was it easy or difficult to think about your various support systems? Why? **(5 marks)**

_____

_____

_____

_____

_____

_____

_____

_____

_____

In Carly's video she mentioned the themes of youth empowerment, post-secondary transitions, and financial responsibility. Where do these themes appear in your own life? How do these themes make you feel? **(5 marks)**

_____

_____

_____

_____

_____

_____

_____

_____

_____

Lesson One: Sateana Goupil

Activity: Mentorship Presentations

CURRICULUM CONNECTIONS	**Alberta, Northwest Territories and Nunavut:** • Aboriginal Studies Grades 10-12 • Career and Life Management Grades 10-12 • English Language Arts Grades 10-12 • English Language Arts Grades 10, 11 and 12: Uqausiliriniq Strand • Health and Life Skills Grade 9 • Knowledge and Employability ELA Grades 10-12 **British Columbia and Yukon:** • Career-Life Education Grades 10-12 • Career-Life Connections Grades 10-12 • Contemporary Indigenous Studies Grade 12 • English Language Arts Composition Grades 10, 11 and 12 • English Language Arts First Peoples Grade 12 **Ontario:** • First Nations, Metis, and Inuit Studies Grades 9-12 • English Language Arts Grades 9-10 • English Language Arts Grades 11-12
DURATION	1-2 hours
OVERVIEW	In this lesson, students will explore topics such as role models, mentorship, leadership, giving back to the community, and coaching. Students will watch Sateana Goupil's Fireside Chat interview in which Sateana discusses his work as a skilled trade journeyman electrician and is a former hockey player. Students will do a rotational graffiti activity about different topics surrounding mentorship. Afterwards they will present their findings from the activity. To summarize the students' learning, they will complete a reflection writing activity answering two self-reflection questions. Students will be assessed by a peer-feedback group assessment form based on how well they worked in their groups.

MATERIALS	• Six large chart or poster papers
	• Six different colours of markers (each group will have their own colour. So enough coloured markers for each group)
	• Example:
	   ○ 5 red markers
	   ○ 5 blue markers
	   ○ 5 black markers
	   ○ 5 green markers
	   ○ 5 purple markers
	   ○ 5 orange markers
	• Whiteboard and whiteboard markers
	• Pencils and looseleaf paper or computer-access for reflection writing
	• "Group Evaluation" Handout
	• "Reflection Writing Assessment Rubric"

ACTIVATE: MENTORSHIP MINDMAP

To begin the lesson, write the word MENTORSHIP in the middle of the white board. Instruct students to open their notebooks or to take a piece of paper out and that you will be working as a class to create a mind map about the word MENTORSHIP. As a class, come up with different subtopics, words, definitions, and connections. The size of the mind map is up to the teacher's discretion.

Subtopic Ideas:

- *Characteristics of a Mentor*
- *Examples of Mentors*
- *Mentees*
- *Community*
- *Jobs that use Mentorship*

ACQUIRE: SATEANA GOUPIL'S FIRESIDE CHAT VIDEO

https://www.firesidechats.ca/video/sateana-goupil

Sateana Goupil is an Inuit man from Kivalliq, Nunavut. He's lived in various places across Canada such as Quebec and Ontario, as well as in the United States in places such as Kansas and Connecticut. Sateana is an electrician and a former hockey player. He became interested in the trade when he was living in Wichita, Kansas, where his partner at the time had a family friend that worked at a construction electrical company. Sateana is still involved in hockey and coaches children. He feels he was very fortunate to be given opportunities to play on high-level teams and learn from excellent coaches during his career, so he felt it was important to give back.

Start the video of Sateana Goupil's interview with Fireside Chats.

To debrief the video, ask the class the following questions:

1. What was one of Sateana's major obstacles? How did he overcome this?
2. How is Sateana still involved with hockey?
3. How does mentorship and coaching help youth for their future?

Since Sateana talked a lot about the importance of mentorship and coaching, students will do a rotational graffiti activity to summarize their prior knowledge and connect their ideas to the content they learned today through the mind mapping activity and knowledge they learned from Sateana Goupil's interview. Afterwards, students will apply their knowledge with a writing activity.

APPLY: MENTORSHIP ROTATIONAL GRAFFITI AND SELF REFLECTION

Students will perform a rotational graffiti to summarize the overall learning from today's lesson. Divide students into 5-6 teams with 3-4 students in each group. Each team will be designated to a different station to start the activity. Distribute a sheet of chart paper to each station and the same-coloured marker for each team member.

Possible Rotational Graffiti Stations:

**Teachers may make up their own stations as well

- Mentorship
- Responsibilities of Mentees
- Leadership

- Characteristics of a Mentor
- Examples of a Mentor
- The Role of Elders in Indigenous Communities
- Giving Back to the Community

Teams can either write or draw as many ideas, concepts, terms, or responses they can think of. This part is done for a short amount of time, such as 2 minutes. Once their time is up, teams will rotate to the next station. Teams will now repeat the same process at each station. Teams will rotate until they have contributed to every station. Eventually, every team will get back to their original station.

Back at their original stations, teams will read and review all the contributions made. Lastly, teams will work to summarize all the ideas written on their sheet. Members may look for main ideas, supporting ideas, overlapping ideas, similarities and/or differences. As a team, they will form a summary statement of their station. Each team will then present their summary statement to the whole class. Presentations should only be around 1-2 minutes long.

ASSESS: GROUP EVALUATION

After students are done presenting, handout the "Group Evaluation Form". Each student will provide feedback to their teacher about how well each member in their group worked and give them a score out of 15.

Next, assign the following questions as a self-reflective paragraph writing assignment. Students will use the following questions to reflect back on their learning, apply the new concepts to their own life, and make connections between knowledge from class and the real world.

Reflection Writing Questions:
1. Who is a mentor in your life and why do you consider them a mentor? Explain what skills and values they may have helped you develop.
2. Have any mentors in your life impacted on what career you want to do one day? Explain.

The mind mapping is a form of formative assessment. Teachers will be able to check students' prior knowledge about mentorship, roles of mentors, leadership, and roles of Elders. Teachers can assess group learning and student communication skills.

The debriefing questions after Sateana's interview with Fireside Chats is a form of formative assessment. Teachers will be able to check what students took away from Santeana's video and make connections to the other parts of the lesson.

The Mentorship Rotational Graffiti Presentations is a summative assessment. Students will be assessed through peer group evaluation. Each student will give each member of their group a mark out of 15. Students will evaluate each other's work ethic during the rotational graffiti stage, creating the summary, and how well they worked together.

The reflection writing is a summative assessment. Students will be assessed by the teacher through a reflection writing rubric. Students will be given a mark out of 15.

TAKE STUDENT LEARNING FURTHER

Activity: Elder Classroom Visit

For students who are showing a keen interest in the topic of mentors, you may want to invite an Elder to the classroom to speak about leadership, mentorship, or how they pass on knowledge. Elders are very important members of Indigenous communities. In Anishinaabe and Red River Metis communities, Elders are seen as knowledge keepers and are highly respected. The term Elder refers to someone who has attained a high degree of understanding of their communities history, traditional teachings, ceremonies, and more. Elders have earned the right to pass on their knowledge and to give advice and guidance.

When inviting an Elder to your classroom, there are certain protocols you must follow. School divisions and districts may have their own Elder Protocols that should be followed.

Elder Protocol Resources

- The Alberta Teachers Association Elder Protocol
- Learn Alberta Elder Wisdom in the Classroom
- Arrow Lakes Aboriginal Education Advisory Council, British Columbia
- School District 8 Kootenay Lake, British Columbia
- Cultural Protocols, Guidelines for Working with Inuit Elders, Nunavut
- Yukon First Nations Protocols
- Elder/Senator Protocol for Schools, Ontario
- University of Toronto, Elder Invitation Protocol, Ontario

GROUP EVALUATION FORM:

On this evaluation form, you will give each person in your group a mark out of 15.

5 = Excellent work; was a crucial component to the group's success.
4 = Very strong work; contributed significantly to the group.
3 = Sufficient effort; contributed adequately to the group.
2 = Insufficient effort; met minimal standards of the group.
1 = Little or weak effort; was detrimental to the group.

	PEER ASSESSMENT (PARTNER 1:_____)
	Participation in the rotational graffiti for each heading
	Participation in creating the summary for your original heading
	Cooperation with other group members
/15	Marks

	PEER ASSESSMENT (PARTNER 2: _____)
	Participation in the rotational graffiti for each heading
	Participation in creating the summary for your original heading
	Cooperation with other group members
/15	Marks

	PEER ASSESSMENT (PARTNER 3:_____)
	Participation in the rotational graffiti for each heading
	Participation in creating the summary for your original heading
	Cooperation with other group members
/15	Marks

	PEER ASSESSMENT (PARTNER 4: _____)
	Participation in the rotational graffiti for each heading
	Participation in creating the summary for your original heading
	Cooperation with other group members
/15	Marks

REFLECTION WRITING ASSESSMENT RUBRIC:

Student Name: _____

CATEGORIES OF PERFORMANCE:	BEGINNER (0)	BASIC (1)	INTERMEDIATE (2)	ADVANCED (3)
Opening sentence	The sentence is incomplete and does not state the main idea.	The sentence is complete, but does not state the main idea.	The sentence is complete and adequately states the main idea.	The sentence is complete and clearly states the main idea.
Supporting sentences	Some sentences are incomplete or run-on and do not support the main idea.	Some sentences are incomplete or run-on, but support the main idea.	Most sentences are complete and support the main idea.	All sentences are complete and support the main idea.
Closing sentence	The sentence is incomplete and does not sum up the paragraph.	The sentence is complete, but does not sum up the paragraph.	The sentence is complete and adequately sums up the paragraph.	The sentence is complete and clearly sums up the paragraph.
Organization of ideas	Ideas in the reflection are disorganized and do not support the main idea, causing a confusion of meaning.	A few ideas in the reflection do not support the main idea or are out of place, causing a confusion of meaning.	Ideas in the reflection support the main idea, but could be organized more clearly.	Ideas flow in the reflection and clearly support the main idea, creating meaning.
Spelling, capitalization, and punctuation	There are many errors in spelling, capitalization, and punctuation.	There are some errors in spelling, capitalization, and punctuation.	There are only a few errors in spelling, capitalization, and punctuation.	There are no errors in spelling, capitalization, or punctuation

/15

Lesson Two: Raven Beardy

Activity: Positive Indigenous Womxn Role Model Research Project

CURRICULUM CONNECTIONS	**Alberta, Northwest Territories and Nunavut:** • Aboriginal Studies Grades 10-12 • English Language Arts Grades 10-12 • English Language Arts Grades 10, 11 and 12: Uqausiliriniq Strand **British Columbia and Yukon:** • Contemporary Indigenous Studies Grade 12 • English Language Arts Composition Grades 10, 11 and 12 • English Language Arts First Peoples Grade 12 **Ontario:** • First Nations, Metis, and Inuit Studies Grades 9-12: • English Language Arts Grades 9-10: • English Language Arts Grades 11-12:
DURATION	2-3 hours
OVERVIEW	In this lesson, students will explore the topics of female representation in male-dominated workforces, womxn leadership, positive role models, and long-term goal setting. Students will watch Raven Beardy's interview with Fireside Chats in which Raven talks about her journey becoming a pilot and working in a male-dominated, non-Indigenous dominated industry. Students will complete a research project on Indigenous Womxn who have made an impact in their communities and/or are strong positive role models. Students will be assessed using a research project rubric. Note: The word "womxn" is an alternative spelling to the word woman, in which the "man" or "men" part is removed. "Womxn" is an intersectional term intended to signal the inclusion of those who have traditionally been excluded from white feminist discourse such as BIPOC (Black, Indigenous, People of Colour) as well as trans-women.
MATERIALS	• Half sheet of white or lined paper per student • Writing instruments (pencil or pen) • Computer access • Indigenous Womxn Role Model Research Project handout • Indigenous Womxn Role Model Research Project assessment rubric

Lesson Plan

☀ ACTIVATE: PAPER AIRPLANE CLASS DISCUSSION

***If students are not familiar with the term "Womxn", begin the lesson with the definition stated above.**

To begin the lesson, tell students that today you will be looking into careers that are typically male-dominated and the importance of female representation in such careers. First, students will think about examples of a strong (resilient, hardworking, achieving) female, or womxn, role model in their life. It can be a family member, a staff member, someone on television or in a movie, etc. A female/womxn role model is a person that people look up to and serves as a positive example to others. Inform students that In this lesson, they will be focussing on womxn who are role models to all. Unfortunately, many industries are male dominated. The lack of female representation can lead womxn to believe that career or industry is not for them.

Hand out a half sheet of white or lined paper to each student. Tell students that on this piece of paper, they will write their example of a female/womxn role model.

After students have written an example of a female/womxn role model they will fold their paper into a paper airplane. In a hallway or from the front to back of the classroom, students will throw their airplanes. Then, everyone will go collect a different airplane and read the responses out loud. The teacher will then record the responses on the board. If students are feeling keen, they may share why they believe this person is an example of a role model.

ACQUIRE: RAVEN BEARDY'S FIRESIDE CHAT VIDEO

https://www.firesidechats.ca/video/raven-beardy-jenvenne

Raven Beardy is a Métis woman from Shamattawa First Nation, located in Northern Manitoba. Raven has also lived in other northern communities such as Grise Fiord, Pond Inlet, and Cambridge Bay. Growing up in the isolated community of Shamattawa, the only way to get anything was by plane. From a young age, Raven would watch the medevac and her interest in planes was sparked. Raven highlights the ways she powered through discouraging times, and different role models that she looked up to. Raven has achieved a lot of her goals, and says the hardworking people in her life such as her grandparents and seeing their work ethic helped her, along with her parents.

Start the video of Raven Beardy's interview with Fireside Chats.

To debrief the video, ask the class the following questions:

1. The aviation industry is male-dominated and non-Indigenous-dominated. How does this affect Raven's career?
2. What does female representation and leadership mean to you?
3. Why are role models important?

Students will use the information learned from Raven's interview, their thoughts with the debriefing questions, and the role model examples discussed in the paper airplane activity to complete a research project outlining a positive Indigenous womxn role model.

APPLY: POSITIVE INDIGENOUS WOMXN ROLE MODEL RESEARCH PROJECT

Students will complete a research project on the life of an Indigenous womxn who makes a positive impact in our society, either historically or presently. For this research project students will construct a timeline that displays their findings. Students will research significant events in the life of the role model. Students must include a minimum of 5 achievements, facts or events on their timelines.

Timelines may be created using the medium of their choice. Medium ideas include: PowerPoint, Poster, Image cards, Website, etc. Students will submit their idea for their role model to the teacher for approval. The student must be able to do online, book, or interview research on their role model.

The timelines should include:

Womxn's name, birthdate, and the type of background/Indigenous they identify as (First Nations, Metis, Inuit, Mixed Indigenous, Biracial, Multiracial etc.), their home community and the community they live in now.

Plus:

- **Five** significant achievements, events or facts about the womxn and when they occurred.
- **Five** images (either hand drawn, digitally created, or photos from the internet that are cited)

ASSESS:

The paper airplane class discussion is a form of formative assessment. Teachers will be able to check students' prior knowledge about what a strong womxn role model is and looks like. Teachers can assess group learning and student communication skills.

The debriefing questions after Raven's interview with Fireside Chats is a form of formative assessment. Teachers will be able to check what students took away from Raven's video and make connections to the other parts of the lesson.

The Positive Indigenous Womxn Role Model Research Project is a summative assessment. Students will be assessed through a research project assessment rubric and be provided with teacher feedback. Students will be assessed by their content, organization, creativity, use of images, and spelling/grammar. Students will be given a mark out of 15 and be provided with teacher feedback.

TAKE STUDENT LEARNING FURTHER

Activity: (Indigenous) Womxn Role Model Interview

For students who are showing a keen interest in the topic of Indigenous womxn role models and leadership, have students complete an interview with a womxn they find inspiring. The womxn could be Indigenous or non-Indigenous. Students can come up with questions individually or as a group that they would ask during their interviews. Students can present the information learned in the interview through an oral presentation, poster, video, or multimedia presentation.

Image created by Ruby Bruce, *Zhaawenoodin*

Introduction:

For this project, you will be creating a timeline outlining achievements, events, or facts about an Indigenous womxn role model that you think is making a positive impact in our society. The role model may have made impacts historically or presently. You will research **five** achievements, events, or facts about your chosen role model. You will put your research in order of date/when it occurred.

You will research using the internet, books, or through interviews. You will present the information through a PowerPoint, Poster, Multimodal presentation, image cards, etc. Please run your ideas by the teacher first. You will need to submit your idea for your Indigneous womxn role model for approval

Definition:

The word "womxn" is an alternative spelling to the word woman, in which the "man" or "men" part is removed. "Womxn" is an intersectional term intended to signal the inclusion of those who have traditionally been excluded from white feminist discourse such as BIPOC (Black, Indigenous, People of Colour) as well as trans-women.

Information to be Included:

1. Womxn's name, birthdate, and the type of background/Indigenous they identify as.
   (First Nations, Metis, Inuit, Mixed Indigenous, Biracial, Multiracial etc.)
2. Home community and community they live in now.
3. **Five** significant achievements, events or facts about the womxn and when they occurred.
   - A significant life event may be moving to the city from their reserve to pursue education and the experience surrounding the big life change.
   - An achievement may be their first march, an award they won, finishing post-secondary, getting their dream career, etc.
4. Add **five** images for each research point.
   - Either hand drawn, digitally created, or photos from the internet that are cited.

POSITIVE INDIGENOUS WOMXN ROLE MODEL RESEARCH PROJECT ASSESSMENT RUBRIC

Student Name: _____

CATEGORIES OF PERFORMANCE:	BEGINNER (0)	BASIC (1)	INTERMEDIATE (2)	ADVANCED (3)
Content	Lots of information is missing. Only one event/achievement was included and not accurate	Some information is missing. Only 2-3 events/achievements were included and/or accurate	Some information is missing. Only 3-4 events/achievements were included and/or accurate.	Name, birthdate, community, background, and 5+ events/achievements are all included and accurate.
Organization	Timeline is not organized. No dates are shown.	Timeline is slightly organized. 3-4 events/achievements do not have dates or are not in order.	Timeline is moderately organized. 1 or 2 events/achievements do not have dates or are not in order.	Timeline is well organized. All events/achievements are dated and in order.
Creativity and Design	Research project shows that no time or effort was put into creativity and design.	Minimal time and effort were used for creativity and design of the research project.	Some effort and time were used for the research project. Project is creative and well designed.	Student went above and beyond with the creativity and design of their project.
Graphics/ Images	No graphics or images are presented.	Graphics or images do not go with the accompanying event/achievement and there are less than 2 images. Graphics or images do not go with the accompanying event/achievement and there are less than 2 images.	Graphics or images go well with accompanying events/achievements but there are less than 5 images.	Graphics and images go well with the accompanying event/achievement. There are 5+ images used.
Spelling and Mechanics	More than 10 spelling and/or writing errors are present.	No more than 10 spelling and/or writing errors are present.	No more than 5 spelling and/or writing errors are present.	No spelling errors and all sections of the brochure are free of writing errors.

/15

Teacher Feedback:

Lesson Three: Krista Paul

Activity: Self-Love Self-Portrait Art

CURRICULUM CONNECTIONS	**Alberta, Northwest Territories and Nunavut:** • Art Grades 10-12 • Art 11-21-31 • English Language Arts Grades 10-12 • English Language Arts Grades 10, 11, and 12: Uqausiliriniq Strand **British Columbia and Yukon:** • Art Studio Grades 10, 11 and 12 • English Language Arts Composition Grades 10, 11 and 12 • English Language Arts First Peoples Grade 12 • Media Arts Grades 10, 11 and 12 **Ontario:** • English Language Arts Grades 9-10 • English Language Arts Grades 11-12 • Entrepreneurship Grades 11-12 • Visual Arts Grades 10-12
DURATION	2 hours
OVERVIEW	In this lesson, students will explore the topics of art, self-love, self-discovery and growth mindset. Students will watch Krista Paul's interview with Fireside Chats where Krista explains that she is a hairstylist and makeup artist and works hard to help people feel and look their best while connecting and talking with them. Students will use the concepts learned in Krista's interview and apply the idea of positive habits and growth mindset to create a self-portrait art piece displaying qualities that they love and value about themselves. Students will do a self-assessment afterwards where they will answer three reflection questions about the experience. Students will be assessed by a portrait self-assessment consisting of three reflection questions and a portrait self-assessment rubric.
MATERIALS	• Computer/Projector • Student cell phones/personal devices with internet • White paper • Different kinds of art mediums (pencil crayons, markers, oil paints, etc.) • Pencils • Mirrors • "Self-Portrait Teacher Example" Handout • "Portrait Self-Assessment" Handout • "Portrait Rubric" Handout

Lesson Plan

☀ ACTIVATE: KRISTA PAUL KAHOOT ACTIVATING STRATEGY QUESTIONS

To begin the lesson, open the Kahoot Game: Would You Rather - Fireside Chat. Listed below are the ten questions on the Kahoot for the activating strategy. If teachers are unable to play online, then the teacher can just ask the questions out loud.

• Would you rather have green hair or have grey hair?
• Would you rather be bald for the rest of your life or never be able to cut your hair again?
• Would you rather only be able to dress in all purple or all white?
• Would you rather only wear crocs or only wear winter boots for a year?

- Would you rather have hair like Rapunzel or hair like Mr. Clean?
- Would you rather be 7 feet tall or 7 inches tall?
- Would you rather have no teeth or have teeth but every time you bite something - your teeth cry?
- Would you rather go to a hair salon or a nail salon?
- Would you rather have to go to school matching with your teacher or matching with a friend?
- Would you rather wear blue eyeliner or bright orange blush?

ACQUIRE: KRISTA PAUL'S FIRESIDE CHAT VIDEO

https://www.firesidechats.ca/video/krista-paul

Krista Paul is a Metis woman and mother of two, from Saskatoon in Treaty 6 territory. Krista \ has been involved in the hair industry since 2009. Krista believes in the power of make-up and styling to enhance people's natural beauty and to bring out their confidence. Krista is passionate about her career and is committed to constantly educating herself with the latest products, techniques and skills for her clients.

Start the video of Krista's interview with Fireside Chats.

To debrief the video, ask the class the following questions:

1. How did Krista reinvigorate her passion for hairstyling?
2. Why did Krista become a hairstylist?
3. Krista talked about people outgrowing their environments. What are some reasons why people change their environments?

Students will use the concepts learned in Krista's interview and apply the idea of positive habits and growth mindset to create a self-portrait art piece displaying things that they love about themselves and an art piece that depicts themselves in a positive way.

APPLY: SELF-LOVE SELF-PORTRAIT ART

Students will create a self-portrait that highlights features they love and value about themselves and depict themselves in a positive light. It can be very hard to love ourselves with negative depictions across social media, the negativity behind body dysmorphia, and the impacts of eurocentric/western beauty trends have on youth. This activity serves to reinforce the idea that everyone is beautiful and our positive qualities should be celebrated.

Students will use either their choice of art style/medium or one chosen by their teachers. How students create the self-portrait art is at the teacher's discretion (drawing, graphic art, painting, collage, etc).

Provide students with mirrors so they can view themselves as they create. Show the "Self-Portrait Teacher Example" to the class so students can get an idea of what they are creating.

The minimum students must draw would be of themself from the neck up. Students can go as far as drawing their entire body. The students must ensure they are being respectful with their drawings. In their self portrait, students will need to use colour, creativity, and show that they put effort and time into their art piece. Students must include 15-20 words describing something that they love or value about themselves.

Example:

- I love my hair, my hair colour, my hair length, my eyes, my eye shape, my eye colour, my height, my smile, my laugh, my voice.
- My best qualities are that I am passionate, strong willed, silly, humorous, resilient, kind, good in school, and a great friend.

ASSESS: SELF-ASSESSMENT QUESTIONNAIRE

Students will complete a self-assessment afterwards where they will answer three reflection questions about the experience. Students will talk about the challenge of creating a self-portrait, what features of themselves they love and highlighted in their piece, and ways they can continue, or start to, love themselves more. Next, students will give themselves a final mark out of 16 based on their self-portrait and self-reflection questions.

The classroom poll is a form of formative assessment. Teachers will be able to check students' prior knowledge about what careers they think relate to Mother Earth, how some jobs can negatively impact Earth, and how some jobs can positively impact Earth. Teachers can assess group learning and student communication skills.

The debriefing questions after Krista's interview with Fireside Chats is a form of formative assessment. Teachers will be able to check what students took away from Krista's video and make connections to the other parts of the lesson.

The Self-Love Self-Portrait Art is a summative assessment. Students will be assessed through a portrait self-assessment. Students will write three reflection questions and be assessed with a portrait rubric. Where the students will give themselves a mark. It is up to the teacher's discretion if they change the mark the student gave themselves. Students will give themselves a final mark out of 16. 12 marks will be allocated to their physical self-portrait and 4 marks to the self-reflection questions.

TAKE STUDENT LEARNING FURTHER

Activity: Self-Care Challenge

For students who are showing a keen interest in the topics of self-love, growth-mindset and self-discovery, students may create a self-care challenge. Using a weekly or monthly calendar, students will plan a way they are going to care for themselves every day.

For example, if doing a week-long self-care challenge:

- Monday - Bubble bath
- Tuesday - Read a book
- Wednesday - Cook my favourite meal for supper
- Thursday - Go on a nature walk
- Friday - Meditate for 30 minutes
- Saturday - Take a 30 minute nap
- Sunday - Make my favourite banana bread

Students can then self-reflect after the week or month is done. They could highlight the challenges and benefits they experienced, if they did a self-care activity every day, and what self-care techniques they want to continue in the future.

SELF-PORTRAIT TEACHER EXAMPLE:

This self-portrait example is using the art medium - digital art. This art piece was created using Procreate on an Apple iPad. The self-portrait shows 19 various describing words.

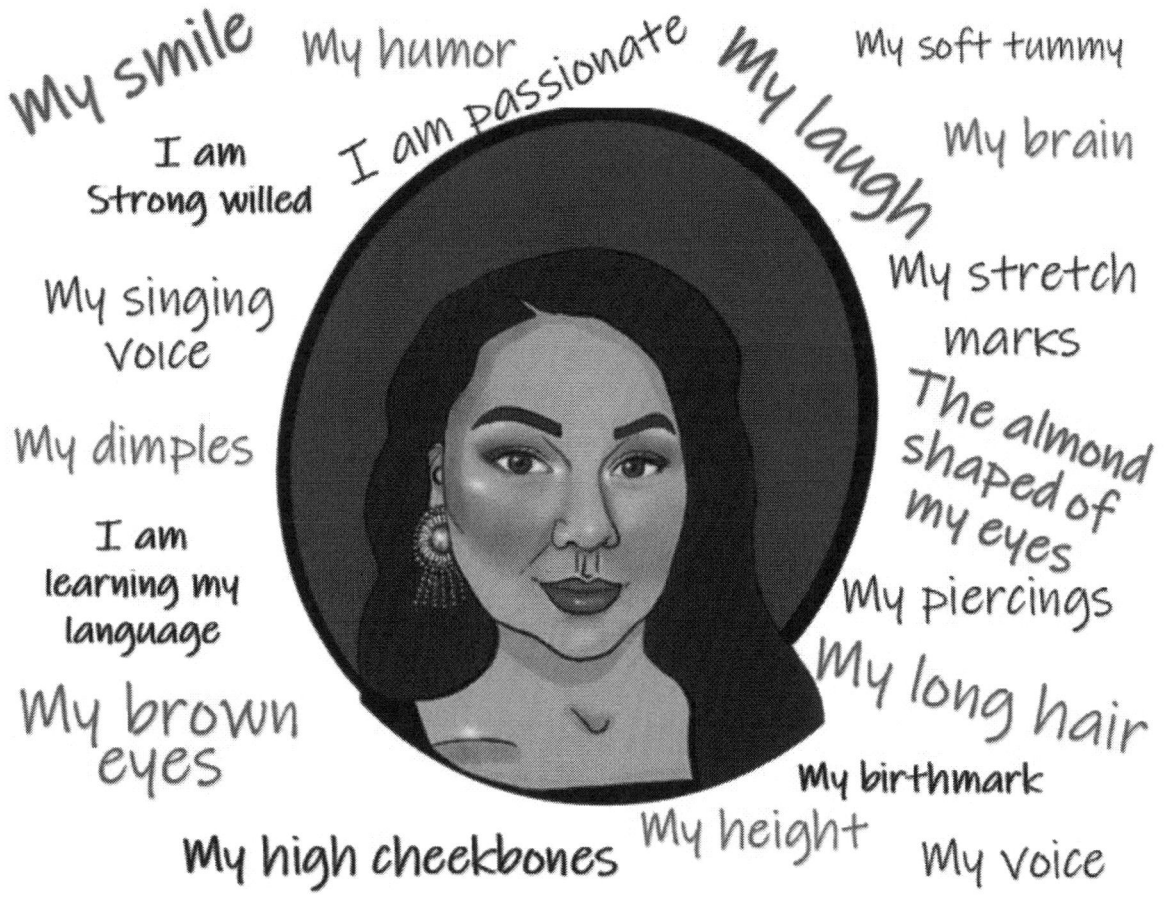

My smile   My humor   I am passionate   My laugh   My soft tummy

I am Strong willed   My brain

My singing voice   My stretch marks

My dimples   The almond shaped of my eyes

I am learning my language   My piercings

My brown eyes   My long hair

My birthmark

My high cheekbones   My height   My voice

This graphic was created by Ruby Bruce and Marika Schalla.

SELF-PORTRAIT SELF-ASSESSMENT:

Below you will self-reflect on your experience creating a self-portrait and then figuring out words to describe things that you love and value about yourself. Answer each question in full sentences.

1. What features of yourself, that you love and valued, did you showcase? Explain why you chose 3 of them.

_____

_____

_____

_____

_____

_____

_____

_____

2. What are some strategies that you can start, or continue, to love parts of yourself more?

_____

_____

_____

_____

_____

_____

_____

_____

3. What are two challenges you faced while creating your self-portraits?

_____

_____

_____

_____

_____

_____

_____

_____

SELF-PORTRAIT ASSESSMENT RUBRIC:

Read through the following assessment rubric for the self-portrait. Give yourself a mark for each category by either adding a checkmark or highlighting the box. Add your values at the end and give yourself a final mark. It is up to the teacher's discretion if marks are changed.

Name: _____

CATEGORIES OF PERFORMANCE:	NEEDS IMPROVE-MENT (1)	GOOD (2)	GREAT (3)	OUTSTANDING (4)
Time and Effort	Class time was not used wisely, and there was no additional effort.	Class time was not always used wisely, but I did do some additional work at home.	Class time was used wisely. I could have put in more time and effort at home.	Much time and effort went into the planning and design. I put in a lot of work at home as well as at school. Much time and effort went into the planning and design. I put in a lot of work at home as well as at school.
Creativity and Design	The project lacked creativity, facial features, and words.	The project could have used more creativity or uniqueness. I used a few colours.	Project was very creative. I used different colours and designs.	Project was exceedingly creative. I used a variety of colours and designs. I thought outside of the box!
Love/Value Describing Terms	I added 1-5 describing words that highlight what I love and value about myself.	I added 5-10 describing words that highlight what I love and value about myself.	I added 10-15 describing words that highlight what I love and value about myself.	I added 15-20+ describing words that highlight what I love and value about myself.
Self Reflection Questions	I barely answered one question. I did not put any effort into my answers.	I answered one question. I put in effort and wrote 3-5 sentences.	I answered two questions. I put in effort and wrote 3-5 sentences.	I answered all three questions. I put in effort and wrote 3-5 sentences.

/16

Lesson One: Mumilaaq Qaqqaq
Activity: Mock Class Debate

CURRICULUM
CONNECTIONS

Alberta, Northwest Territories and Nunavut:
- Aboriginal Studies Grades 10-12
- English Language Arts Grades 10-12
- English Language Arts Grades 10, 11, 12: Uqausiliriniq Strand
- Social Studies Grades 10,11, 12
- Social Studies Grades 10,11, 12: Nunavusiutit
- Aulajaaqtut Grades 10, 11, 12

British Columbia and Yukon:
- Contemporary Indigenous Studies Grade 12
- English Language Arts Composition Grades 10, 11, 12
- English Language Arts First Peoples Grade 12
- Exploration in Social Studies Grade 11
- Law Studies Grade 12
- Political Studies Grade 12
- Social Justice Grade 12
- Social Studies Grade 10

Ontario:
- Canadian and International Politics, University Preparation, Grade 12
- Civics (Politics) Grade 10
- First Nations, Metis, and Inuit Studies Grades 9-12
- English Language Arts Grades 9-10
- English Language Arts Grades 11-12
- Equity, Diversity, and Social Justice, Grade 11
- Equity and Social Justice, From Theory to Practice, Grade 12
- Issues in Canadian Geography, Applied, Grade 9
- Politics in Action, Open, Grade 11
- The Environment and Resource Management, Grade 12

DURATION

1 hour

OVERVIEW

In this lesson, students will explore the topics of Inuit leadership, impacts of Indigenous representation in Parliament, and social issues impacting Indigenous and northern communities. Students will watch a video of Mumilaaq Qaqqaq's final House of Commons speech. In her speech, Mumilaaq talks about how she did not feel safe or how she belonged in Parliament. The video is an empowering, thought-provoking speech about the microaggressions that Inuit people (and other BIPOC people) face in politics.

Students will watch Mumilaaq Qaqqaq's interview with Fireside Chats. Mumilaaq Qaqqaq is an Inuk woman, Member of Parliament, and human rights defender. Elected in 2019, Mumilaaq recently (June 2021) announced that she will not be running for re-election. Mumilaaq has been fighting for adequate housing, clean water and food security in Nunavut and other northern communities in Canada. Students will then participate in a mock debate about clean water in northern communities. Students will be assessed by peer feedback and evaluation, as well as a self-reflection sheet.

MATERIALS

- Computer Access and Projector
- "Group Evaluation" Rubric
- "Peer Evaluation Feedback Form" (Optional)
- "Class Debate Self-Reflection"
- Debate Information Sides A and B Print-Outs (Optional)
- Writing Instruments (Pencils, Pens, etc.)

ACTIVATE: MUMILAAQ QAQQAQ'S FINAL HOUSE OF COMMONS SPEECH

To begin the lesson, instruct the class that today they will be watching two videos featuring Mumilaaq Qaqqaq, a former Member of Parliament for Nunavut, an Inuit leader, and human rights defender. In the first video, they will be watching Mumilaaw's final House of Commons speech. In this farewell, Mumilaaq denounces Canada's racism. She highlights the culture of workplace racism in Parliament and the empty promises that the federal government has made toward Indigenous Peoples. Play the video and have students write down their thoughts, feelings, and emotions that the speech evokes.

To debrief the video, ask the class the following questions:

1. What are some feelings or emotions you felt while listening to Mumilaaq's speech?
2. What barriers do young, marginalized people face when they decide to run for office?

ACQUIRE: MUMILAAQ QAQQAQ'S FIRESIDE CHAT VIDEO

Mumilaaq Qaqqaq (ᒧᒥᓛᖅ ᖃᖅᖃᖅ) is a Member of Parliament, and human rights defender. She is best known for a speech she made in the House of Commons on International Women's Day in 2017. Originally from Baker Lake, Nunavut, she now lives in the capital, Iqaluit. Mumilaaq is the elected MP for Nunavut and former employment officer with Nunavut Tunngavik Incorporated. She previously worked as a Wellness Program Specialist with the health department of the Government of Nunavut. She has held positions with Inuit Tapariit Kanatami, Susan Aglukark, and Northern Youth Abroad. As a youth leader with connections across the territory, Mumilaaq knows how important it is to recognize the unique culture of Nunavut communities and the distinct challenges Nunavummiut face. Mumilaaq is standing with Jagmeet Singh and the NDP to improve the lives of Nunavummiut, through affordable housing, better access to services, and federal laws that are in harmony with the United Nations Declaration on the Rights of Indigenous Peoples.

Start the video of Mumilaaq Qaqqaq's interview with Fireside Chats. In the interview, Mumilaaq discusses her career and education journey to become a Member of Parliament for Nunavut.

To debrief the video, ask the class the following questions:

1. What does Mumilaaq label as her biggest barrier/worst-critic and why?
2. What advice does Mumilaaq have for her younger self?
3. What is the importance in having Mumilaaq pave the way for other Indigenous youth to be heard?

Students will use the knowledge and teachings from both of the videos featuring Mumilaaq and apply them to a Mock Class Debate.

APPLY: MOCK CLASS DEBATE ON ACCESS TO CLEAN WATER

Students will participate in a mock class debate. In this debate, the topic will be about access to clean water in northern communities in Canada. Half of the class will be on the "For" side or "Side A". The other half will be the "Against" side or "Side B".

In a classroom debate, a proposition is stated and students make arguments for or against the statement. Students will be given hand-outs and must research and prepare arguments. Students will be given a large chart paper to write down their arguments and ideas. Students must complete research before they start debating so they can participate in the debate effectively. While debating, students are required to think on the spot and respond to the opposing sides' counterarguments.

Note: In this activity, students may feel different about the side they are debating on. For example, a student may be on the side debating that northern communities should not get funding to access clean drinking water, when the student feels like northern communities should. This is okay, they will be able to reflect on their experience at the end. This activity will help students get an eye-opening experience of the social justice issues happening to Indigenous peoples and northern communities today.

Statement: Funding should be given to northern communities and reserves to help them access to clean drinking water.

Side A (For): Will be the team that believes Northern Communities/Reserves need funding to help them access clean drinking water.

Side B (Against): Will be the team that debates that there is not enough money/resources to give funding for clean drinking water to northern communities.

Split students into two groups. Once students are put into the two groups, have them go to opposite ends of the classroom and hand-out the information for their side. Side A will get the Side A Information and Side B will get the Side B information. Give students about 5-10 minutes to read through their information. After reading, students can write out arguments that they have, and ideas or thoughts they came up with about the topic. After writing, students can choose leaders to present the arguments and counterarguments.

The information sheets are optional to use. Teachers are welcome to use information they already have or create their own!

During the debate, the teacher should monitor the time limits and the direction that the debate is going. At this point in the activity, the teacher is more of a facilitator and guide.

There are many ways to structure a debate. An example of a traditional debate structure:

- Opening "For" Statement - Side A (5 minutes)
- Rebuttal from "Against" - Side B (3 minutes)
- Opening "Against" Statement - Side B (5 minutes)
- Rebuttal from "For" - Side A (3 minutes)
- Teams question each other (5 minutes per team)
- Closing statements from the "Against" - Side B (3 minutes)
- Closing statements from the "For" - Side A (3 minutes)

The teacher should also monitor student participation and check to see which students are collaborating with their group, if any students are not participating, and if any students are talking over others. Teachers can track student cooperation and the contributions they are making to the debate.

When the debate is over, the teacher can open up the debate to comments to hear more perspectives from all students. Students may share if they have any other information that was not shared in the debate. Ask if any students minds' were changed by the statements made today in class and to explain why.

Finally, students can vote to indicate which side presented the most convincing argument and should "win" the debate. Ask students to raise their hands for the statements made by the For and Against sides.

ASSESS:

The video about Mumilaaq Qaqqaq is a form of formative assessment. This activity is to activate students' minds and get the class thinking of Inuit leadership, and social justice issues impacting Indigenous and northern communities. Teachers can check student thinking, and assess their analytical and communication skills.

The debriefing questions after Mumilaaq's interview with Fireside Chats is a form of formative assessment. Teachers will be able to check what students took away from Raven's video and make connections to the other parts of the lesson.

The Mock Class Debate is a summative assessment. Students will be assessed by a group evaluation rubric, peer feedback evaluation, a debate self assessment question and a self-assessment rubric. The self-assessment rubric is for students to give themselves a meaningful mark for their contributions and experience.

TAKE STUDENT LEARNING FURTHER

Activity: Letter to an MP Writing Activity

To take students' learning further, if they are keen on social justice issues they may write a letter to their Member of Parliament. In the students' letters, they may write about a specific issue they want to be addressed or to learn more about. Letters should be no more than a page long. In the letter students would need to state the purpose/objective of the letter at the beginning and briefly introduce the concerns they have.

Next, students should describe why they are interested in the issue. Students may include questions to ask their MP for more information on the issue and/or their stance. Finally, students could make a request for a specific action to be taken, and explain why this action is important. Students can also give thanks to their MP for any positive action they have taken in the past on the issue they are presenting.

GROUP EVALUATION RUBRIC

CATEGORIES OF PERFORMANCE:	NEEDS IMPROVE-MENT (1)	GOOD (2)	GREAT (3)	OUTSTANDING (4)
Effort and Participation	Little or no evidence of participation; no effort shown	Minimal effort; superficial knowledge even after researching; minimal effort	Fully prepared; Participated well. Effort was competent, but not extraordinary	Worked as a leader for the group; extraordinary effort demonstrated
Contribution	Very poor contribution.; little, if any, contribution to the research and the debate	Poor contribution. some contributions to the group but not much.	Good quality of contribution to the group. Worked well with everyone.	Outstanding contribution; above-and-beyond; work is excellent in form and substance
Attitude and Behaviour	Negative Attitude: The peer was withdrawn, absent, or had a negative attitude and behaviour during the research and the debate.	Neutral; The peer was neither encouraging nor discouraging; disinterested in the performance of others during the research and the debate.	Positive; The peer was supportive; mostly constructive and upbeat during the research and the debate.	Exceptionally positive and constructive; encourages other group members during the research and the debate.

GROUP MEMBER NAME	EFFORT AND PARTICIPATION /4	CONTRIBUTION /4	ATTITUDE AND BEHAVIOUR /4	TOTAL /12

PEER FEEDBACK FORM:

Every person in the group needs to have feedback about themselves. Decide amongst your groups who will evaluate who.

Below, you will evaluate two members of your group and write 4-6 sentences for how well your peers participated and collaborated within the group.

You can comment on the person's effort, their communication skills, their cooperation, their participation, things they did well, things they need to improve on etc. This feedback is meant to be constructive feedback. Remain respectful and thoughtful in your responses.

Peer One Name:

_____

_____

_____

_____

_____

_____

_____

_____

_____

Peer Two Name:

_____

_____

_____

_____

_____

_____

_____

_____

_____

CLASS DEBATE SELF-REFLECTION:

Below you will answer a self-reflection question about your experience participating in the mock debate about access to water.

Reflect on your experience with the debate and how the information impacted you. What side were you on? Did you agree with the side you were on? Explain. *(8-10 sentences).*

_____

_____

_____

_____

_____

_____

_____

_____

_____

_____

_____

_____

_____

_____

SIDE A - DEBATE INFORMATION SHEET:

Your team will debate that Northern Communities/Reserves need funding to help them access clean drinking water. There is some information and resources provided below about this topic.

Basic Human Rights:

https://www.unwater.org/water-facts/human-rights/

According to the United Nations, access to potable water and sanitation are human rights. "Lack of access to safe, sufficient and affordable water, sanitation and hygiene facilities has a devastating effect on the health, dignity and prosperity of billions of people, and has significant consequences for the realization of other human rights." (United Nations, 2010)

The Water Crisis:

https://www.cbc.ca/news/politics/auditor-general-reports-2021-1.5927572

The water crisis is the issue of no clean drinking water in Northern and Indigenous communities in Canada. You know how kids can swim in their pools, have water balloon fights and enjoy a glass of homemade iced tea? Well the children who are stuck in water crisis zones can't. Since the tap water in, for example, Ontario First Nation of Attawapiskat isn't safe at all. It has high levels of a chemical byproduct produced by the chlorination process in the community's ailing water plant that needs millions of dollars in repairs. The government does not see this as a top priority.

Safe Water for Indigenous Peoples:

https://canadians.org/fn-water

Water security can be defined as "sustainable access on a watershed basis to adequate quantities of water, of acceptable quality, to ensure human and ecosystem health". This definition sets baseline requirements for water resources management in a watershed on a continuous basis; there must be access to adequate quantities of acceptable quality of water for both humans and the environment.

Shoal Lake 40 First Nation

https://www.youtube.com/watch?v=Arnqpnm70Nq

The citizens of Winnipeg, Manitoba receive their clean potable water from Shoal Lake. Did you know that the lake and community that Winnipeg gets its water from Shoal Lake 40 First Nation. A reserve that is under a boil water advisory. This means they do not have clean potable drinking water. Even though the residents live on the lake where Winnipeggers get their clean water from.

Indigenous Water Governance:

http://decolonizingwater.ca/

Indigenous peoples view water as a living entity to which we have a sacred responsibility to take care of and respect. After all, water is what gives us life. This viewpoint frequently conflicts with Western/Settler views of water as a "resource" that can be owned, managed, and exploited. Organizations like Decolonizing Water wish to create self-sustaining water and ecological monitoring programs that will enhance protection of water resources and fulfill the promise of Indigenous water self-governance.

SIDE B - DEBATE INFORMATION SHEET:

Your team will debate that there is not enough money/resources to give clean drinking water to all northern/reserve communities. There is some information and resources provided below about this topic.

Unrealistic Goals Were Set:
https://www.macleans.ca/news/canada/why-cant-we-get-clean-water-to-first-nation-reserves/

Based on Macleans' research, there have been over 10 years of policies developed from 2001 to 2013, and it's clearly shown that the approaches have not yet made a difference within the First Nations communities. Trudeau's promise to end boil-water advisories within a five-year period is just not a realistic goal. There are over 600 First Nation and northern communities that have issues with water. One approach will not address the issues. There needs to be more individual consultation within each community to find the root of the problem. Each community has a different type of leadership, different geographical location, and different numbers in population. Different geographical location and remoteness means different types of water management are needed. Northern communities need systems to withstand permafrost. Each group needs to set up human resources dedicated to water management. Not all communities have these capacities at the moment.

Water Varies:
https://globalnews.ca/news/5887716/first-nations-boil-water-advisories/

One of the biggest reasons why there are water crises on First Nations, is that there is so many discrepancies between communities of why they do not have clean water. Clean water can be impacted by where it is originating from, the pipes it has to flow through, down to how far the water has to travel to a remote community,

The Government's Capacity:
https://www.sac-isc.gc.ca/eng/1506514143353/1533317130660

Ending a drinking water advisory is often complex, spanning multiple phases. Actions to resolve a water or wastewater issue can include:

- New system design work
- Regular repairs on existing systems
- Permanent repairs to existing infrastructure
- Construction of new infrastructure

Completion of a new water treatment system can take 3 to 4 years on average to complete. Eliminating long-term drinking water advisories is just one part of ensuring First Nations communities have reliable access to safe drinking water.

Not Enough Funds:
https://globalnews.ca/news/7656235/lack-of-funding-for-piped-water-on-first-nations-in-sask-means-some-on-reserves-cant-drink-from-their-taps/

Many reserves do not have the funds to buy and create new water treatment sites, new pipes, and new infrastructure. Peepeekisis Cree Nation, Saskatchewan, needs $8.5 million to connect all their homes by a low-pressure waterline system to a water treatment plant. Indigenous Services Canada would pay some of the costs but it is not feasible, or in the budget, to provide every reserve with large amounts of money. There is not enough money.

Lesson Two: Senator Yvonne Boyer

Activity: Mock Class Election

CURRICULUM
CONNECTIONS

Alberta, Northwest Territories and Nunavut:

- Aboriginal Studies Grades 10-12
- English Language Arts Grades 10-12
- English Language Arts Grades 10, 11, 12: Uqausiliriniq Strand
- Social Studies Grades 10, 11, 12
- Social Studies Grades 10, 11, 12: Nunavusiutit

British Columbia and Yukon:

- Contemporary Indigenous Studies Grade 12
- English Language Arts Composition Grades 10, 11, 12:
- English Language Arts First Peoples Grade 12
- Exploration in Social Studies Grade 11
- Law Studies Grade 12
- Political Studies Grade 12
- Social Justice Grade 12
- Social Studies Grade 10

Ontario:

- Canadian and International Politics, University Preparation, Grade 12
- Civics (Politics) Grade 10
- First Nations, Metis, and Inuit Studies Grades 9-12
- English Language Arts Grades 9-10
- English Language Arts Grades 11-12
- Equity, Diversity, and Social Justice, Grade 11
- Equity and Social Justice, From Theory to Practice, Grade 12
- Issues in Canadian Geography, Applied, Grade 9
- Politics in Action, Open, Grade 11
- The Environment and Resource Management, Grade 12

DURATION

2-3 days

OVERVIEW

In this lesson, students will explore the topics of government, politics, Indigenous representation in federal government systems, and advocacy. Students will participate in an activating activity called Maamawi Island. Maamawi (Maa-ma-wih) is the Anishinaabemowin word for together. In this activity, students will work together to figure out how they will survive as a group on a deserted island; while their teacher is gone to get help. Maamawi Island is an activity to represent democracy and loosely the implications and challenges of government decision making.

Next, students will watch Senator Yvonne Boyers's interview with Fireside Chats. Students will then create their own mock class election in which students will make informed decisions to create their own political party for a mock election. Each group will study electoral procedures while using teamwork and creative thinking skills. Students will get an understanding of politics, the function of government, and parliamentary via the mock election. The experience also helps encourage future young voters to think about who they are voting for and why it is important to vote. Students will be assessed by peer evaluation and a poster rubric.

MATERIALS

- Computer Access for each student
- "Maamawi Island" handout
- "Election Campaign Outline"
- "Poster Rubric"
- "Group Evaluation" Form
- Writing Instruments (Pencils, Pens)
- Poster Paper
- Markers, pencil crayons, permanent markers, etc.

☀ ACTIVATE: MAAMAWI (*MAA-MA-WIH*) ISLAND

To begin the lesson, instruct the students that today we will be looking at government and careers in government. But first, students need to work together to get off Maamawi Island.

Split the class into groups of 3-4 and hand-out the "Maamawi Island" handout. In this exercise students will have to communicate with each other to figure out a few problems after their class is theoretically stuck on a deserted island. In this exercise, students will be figuring out a government system without first realizing it! It is a great activating strategy when talking about government and government systems.

Read the introduction to the class:

Our class is heading on an end-of-year trip across the ocean. Our flight encounters a bad storm, and we become stranded together on a remote island. It will be several weeks until we are rescued. Your teacher (me) and the other adults have decided to travel to the nearest island for help. The class must figure out how everyone will try to live together and survive. With your group, figure out how you will live together and survive by answering the following questions.

Give students approximately 15-20 minutes to answer the questions found on the "Maamawi Island" handout. Walk around the room while they are working to assess participation, group work, communication, critical thinking and problem-solving skills. When groups are done, have one speaker from the group share their answers. Offer alternative answers to questions for students to consider if the groups do not express different answers.

To debrief the activity ask the following questions:

1. How were decisions made for each question? Did everyone agree with the decisions?
2. How do you think this activity relates to the government and being a member of the government?

👤 ACQUIRE: FIRESIDE CHAT WITH SENATOR YVONNE BOYER

https://www.firesidechats.ca/video/senator-yvonne-boyer

Senator Yvonne Boyer is a member of the Métis Nation of Ontario with her ancestral roots in the Métis Nation-Saskatchewan and the Red River. With a background in nursing, including in the operating room, she has over 21 years of experience practicing law and publishing extensively on the topics of Indigenous health and how Aboriginal rights and treaty law intersects on the health of First Nations, Metis and Inuit people. She is a member of the Law Society of Ontario and the Law Society of Saskatchewan and received her Bachelor of Laws from the University of Saskatchewan, and her Master of Laws and Doctor of Laws from the University of Ottawa.

In 2013, she completed a Postdoctoral Fellowship with the Indigenous Peoples' Health Research Centre at the University of Regina. She is a former Canada Research Chair in Aboriginal Health and Wellness at Brandon University. In addition to running her own law practice, she came to the Senate of Canada from the University of Ottawa, where she was the Associate Director for the Centre for Health Law, Policy and Ethics and a part time professor in the Faculty of Law. Senator Boyer is one of eight people from across Canada chosen to be a holographic narrator in the Turning Points for Humanity Gallery at the Canadian Museum for Human Rights in Winnipeg. Her ongoing work has been recognized with numerous awards including a 2018 Honorary Doctorate in Education from Nipissing University.

Start the video of Senator Boyer's interview with Fireside Chats. Alternatively, students can read her story in the textbook or on the web site. In the interview, Senator Boyer discusses her education and career journey as a Senator.

To debrief the video, ask the class the following questions:
1. What was the turning point in Senator Boyer's life/career?
2. What laws does Senator Boyer state are more powerful than the Western Law of the Constitution?
3. What advice does Senator Boyer give to young people who are questioning what they should be doing in life?

Next, students will use the learning from the Maamawi Island activity, and teachings from Senator Boyer in her fireside chat interview, to hold a mock class election!

APPLY: MOCK CLASS ELECTION

Students will work in small groups to form "political parties" and run for class election. Groups will run an election campaign together. Groups will be made of 3-4 people. You may want to make groups at random, let students choose their own groups, or you can take a brief questionnaire and put students with similar political views together.

Groups will first complete the "Election Campaign Outline" handout. This is where they will outline all their ideas for their political party, starting with a name! Remind students to choose a respectful, thoughtful and appropriate name. Next on the worksheet, students will figure out an electoral slogan (*Example: Choose Green for a Better Tomorrow!*), and an electoral statement. The statement should be 1-2 sentences to summarize their election goals. Next, groups will need to make a list of 6 points of how they will make the class better, and one reason why they want to be class leader. After students are finished with their worksheets, check it over and give the group the go ahead to start the next step.

When groups are ready, they will create two different posters for their political party. The posters will show that they are running for election. Posters must include the name of their political party, their electoral slogan, use colour, images/graphics and show creativity, organization and effort. Students may post their posters in the classroom, hallway, or hold them up during their presentation.

Choose a day for groups to present their ideas to the class. Students will present their name, electoral slogan, electoral statement, ways they will make the classroom better and the reason why they should be chosen to be Class Leader.

Optional: Voting. After the presentation of political parties, students will vote for which party they want to be their class leaders. Students can raise their hands to pick the best group, have a class discussion, or run a voting booth!

ASSESS:

The Survivor Island activity is a form of formative assessment. This activity will enable teachers to assess group learning and student communication skills.

The debriefing questions after Senator Boyer's interview with Fireside Chats is a form of formative assessment. Teachers will be able to check what students took away from the video and make connections to the other parts of the lesson.

The Mock Class Election is a summative assessment. Students will be assessed by peer evaluation, a poster rubric and a self-reflection on the group evaluation.

TAKE STUDENT LEARNING FURTHER

Activity: Media Construction of Political Campaign Analysis
To take students' learning further, students can analyze the way the media portrays various political parties and how the media shapes perception of different political campaigns. Political campaigns include Presidential campaigns, Prime Minister campaigns, National First Nation Chief campaigns, Member of Parliament campaigns, etc. Students will look at the discrepancies between political parties and the influence media has on society when there is an election afoot. Students may complete a presentation, group project, oral report, multimedia presentation etc to share their findings.

MAAMAWI ISLAND

Our class is heading on a trip across the ocean! Sadly, our flight encountered a bad storm, and we became stranded together on a remote island. We find an old broken sign saying "Maamawi Island". Since we are so far away, it will be several weeks until we are rescued. Your teacher and the other adults have decided to travel to the nearest island for help. You and the class must figure out how everyone will try to live together and survive.

With your group, figure out how you will live together and survive by answering the following questions.

1. How will the class build shelter and find food and water? Will the class work together as a whole team, in small teams or individually? Explain.

2. If your group chose for people to work as a team, or in small groups, how would you divide up the tasks? (Who will get water, who will get food? Is there a schedule or rotation?)

3. Will a leader be chosen from the class to help lead everyone? How will they be chosen? What will be the leader's role and what power will they have over everyone?

4. Are rules necessary? What rules are needed? Who will make the important decisions?

5. What happens to classmates who are not contributing or breaking rules?

ELECTION CAMPAIGN OUTLINE

Political Party Name: _____

Group Members: _____

Election Slogan: _____

In this section, you will come up with a catchphrase or motto for your political party!

Election Goals:

_____

_____

In this section, you will write out 6 goals you have as a political party of how you want to positively change the classroom. At the end, give a summary of why your group deserves to be the class leaders.

1.

2.

3.

4.

5.

6.

Why should your political party be the class leaders?

_____

_____

_____

Electoral Statement:

In this section, you will summarize your election goals into a 1-2 sentence long statement.

_____

_____

_____

_____

Poster Outline

As a group, you will create two posters. These posters will be a visual for your election campaign.

Posters must include:

- The name of your political party
- You electoral slogan
- Four of your party's goals
- Colour, Images, and Graphics
- Must be able to read the poster from across the classroom
- Use creativity with your design and show that your group put in a lot of effort and time.

Presentations:

After all groups are done making their election campaign and posters, you will present your campaign to the rest of the class!

Presentations must include:

- You Political Party's name,
- You electoral slogan,
- Your electoral statement,
- The 6 ways you will make the classroom better
- Finally, a closing statement to catch the class's attention.

POSTER ASSESSMENT RUBRIC

CATEGORIES OF PERFORMANCE:	NEEDS IMPROVEMENT (1)	GOOD (2)	GREAT (3)	OUTSTANDING (4)
Time and Effort	Class time was not used wisely, and there was no additional effort.	Class time was not always used wisely, but the group did do some additional work at home.	Class time was used wisely. The group could have put in more time and effort at home.	Much time and effort went into the planning and design. The group put in a lot of work at home as well as at school.
Creativity and Design	The project lacked creativity, colour, images and graphics. Could not read from across the room.	The project could have used more creativity or uniqueness. The group used a few colours and images. Could read some things from across the room.	Project was very creative. Usage different colours and images. Can read most of the posters from across the room.	Project was exceedingly creative. Usage of a variety of colours and images. The group thought outside of the box! Can easily read from across the room.
Political Party Name and Slogan	Political Party Name and/or Electoral Slogan were not present.	Political Party Name and/or electoral slogan was hard to see and disorganized	Political Party Name or electoral slogan were present, mostly organized and somewhat easy to notice.	Political Party Name and electoral slogan were present, organized, and easy to nice.
Electoral Campaign Goals	Only one goal was presented neatly and organized on the poster.	Two goals were presented neatly and organized on the poster.	Three goals were presented neatly and organized on the poster.	Four goals were presented neatly on the poster

/16

ELECTORAL POSTER TWO

CATEGORIES OF PERFORMANCE:	NEEDS IMPROVEMENT (1)	GOOD (2)	GREAT (3)	OUTSTANDING (4)
Time and Effort	Class time was not used wisely, and there was no additional effort.	Class time was not always used wisely, but the group did do some additional work at home.	Class time was used wisely. The group could have put in more time and effort at home.	Much time and effort went into the planning and design. The group put in a lot of work at home as well as at school.
Creativity and Design	The project lacked creativity, colour, images and graphics. Could not read from across the room.	The project could have used more creativity or uniqueness. The group used a few colours and images. Could read some things from across the room.	Project was very creative. Usage different colours and images. Can read most of the posters from across the room.	Project was exceedingly creative. Usage of a variety of colours and images. The group thought outside of the box! Can easily read from across the room.
Political Party Name and Slogan	Political Party Name and/or Electoral Slogan were not present.	Political Party Name and/or electoral slogan was hard to see and disorganized	Political Party Name or electoral slogan were present, mostly organized and somewhat easy to notice.	Political Party Name and electoral slogan were present, organized, and easy to nice.
Electoral Campaign Goals	Only one goal was presented neatly and organized on the poster.	Two goals were presented neatly and organized on the poster.	Three goals were presented neatly and organized on the poster.	Four goals were presented neatly on the poster

/16

Total /32

GROUP EVALUATION:

5 = Excellent work; was crucial component to group's success with election campaign

4 = Very strong work; contributed significantly to the group with election campaign

3 = Sufficient effort; contributed adequately to the group and with election campaign

2 = Insufficient effort; met minimal standards of the group with election campaign

1 = Little or weak effort; was detrimental to group and with election campaign

	YOUR NAME:_____
	Participation in choosing the political party name and electoral slogan
	Participation and collaborative in creating the electoral goals
	Participation and collaborative in creating the two election posters
	Cooperation with other group members
	Interest and enthusiasm in the presentation
	Mark out of _____/25

	PEER 1 NAME:_____
	Participation in choosing the political party name and electoral slogan
	Participation and collaborative in creating the electoral goals
	Participation and collaborative in creating the two election posters
	Cooperation with other group members
	Interest and enthusiasm in the presentation
	Mark out of _____/25

	PEER 2 NAME:_____
	Participation in choosing the political party name and electoral slogan
	Participation and collaborative in creating the electoral goals
	Participation and collaborative in creating the two election posters
	Cooperation with other group members
	Interest and enthusiasm in the presentation
	Mark out of _____/25

	PEER 3 NAME:_____
	Participation in choosing the political party name and electoral slogan
	Participation and collaborative in creating the electoral goals
	Participation and collaborative in creating the two election posters
	Cooperation with other group members
	Interest and enthusiasm in the presentation
	Mark out of _____/25

Lesson One: Taylar Belanger

Activity: Western Science and Traditional Ecological Knowledge

CURRICULUM CONNECTIONS	**Alberta, Northwest Territories and Nunavut:** • Aboriginal Studies Grades 10-12 • English Language Arts Grades 10-12 • English Language Arts Grades 10, 11, 12: Uqausiliriniq Strand • Science Grades 11-12 **British Columbia and Yukon:** • Contemporary Indigenous Studies Grade 12 • Earth Sciences Grade 11 • English Language Arts Composition Grades 10, 11, 12 • English Language Arts First Peoples Grade 12 • Environmental Science Grade 12 • Explorations in Social Studies Grade 11 • Life Sciences Grade 11 • Science for Citizens Grade 11 • Social Studies Grades 10 **Ontario:** • English Language Arts Grades 9-10 • English Language Arts Grades 11-12 • Environmental Science Grade 11 • First Nations, Metis, and Inuit Studies Grades 9-12 • Social Studies Grades 9-12 • Science Grades 9-10 • Science Grade 12, University/College Preparation
DURATION	1 hour
OVERVIEW	Throughout this lesson, students will learn about traditional herbalist, Taylar Belanger, while exploring ideas about ecosystem protection, connections in nature, and the difference between western science and traditional Indigenous ecological knowledge. Students will consider the roles and responsibilities that we all have when looking after Mother Earth. Students will write a research essay analyzing the differences and similarities between western science and traditional ecological knowledge. Teachers may want to invite an Elder or traditional knowledge keeper to the classroom to talk about the traditional ecological viewpoint firsthand.
MATERIALS	• Chart paper • Markers • "Aspects of Ecosystems Cut-Outs" handout English or Anishinaabemowin (cut and placed into envelopes per group) • Western Science and Traditional Knowledges Research Essay • Western Science and Traditional Knowledges Rubric • Indigenous Worldview and Traditional Ecological Knowledge Teacher Resource • Computer access

ACTIVATE: SMALL GROUP DISCUSSION

Start the lesson by dividing students into groups of 3-4. Inform them that they will be posed with different questions and dilemmas in their small groups and the goal is that they have to work together to answer the questions as best they can. Hand out one piece of chart paper per group and enough markers for each group member.

1. Have groups number their chart papers 1-4 with lots of space. Ask the first question **"What are some of our roles and responsibilities in looking after (Mother) Earth?"** Allow students time to write down all their answers.
2. Hand-out one "Aspects of Ecosystems Cut-Outs" envelope per group. With the 8 cards in the envelope, ask groups to *rank the words in order of importance*. Go around the room and check students' rankings. Have students list their importance and reason why as **Question 2**. *Do not give them any more context than "importance". Let students think about it and figure out if that means importance in the ecosystem, importance to them, importance in food webs, etc.*
3. Now ask each group to remove the **"Plant"** card. Ask the question "How will removing plants impact the other parts and Earth? Have students write down the question as **Question 3**. Have groups discuss and come up with an answer they can all agree on.
4. Finally, ask each group to remove the **"Person"** card. Ask the question "How will removing people impact the other parts and Earth?" Have students write down the question as **Question 4**. Have groups discuss and come up with an answer they can all agree on.

Once groups have answered the questions to their best abilities, have them walk around and read the answers other groups came up with! Engage in a whole class discussion by asking students what they learned from this activity. Solicit student answers.

Extension: Teachers may continue the exercise by removing more cards. Ask similar questions about what would happen if you removed sun, cloud, rock, moose, bear, and spider from ecosystems.

ACQUIRE: TAYLAR BELANGER'S FIRESIDE CHAT VIDEO

Taylar Belanger, also known as Sōhka, is a traditionalist herbalist and R&B/Hip-hop artist from the northern community of Sakitawak Cree Nation (Ile-a-la-Crosse), Saskatchewan with roots in Ahtahkakoop First Nation. Taylar has always had a strong connection with Mother Earth and plants from a young age. Taylar has been attending Wild Rose College of Natural Healing in Calgary, Alberta in the Practical Herbalist program. Afterwards, Taylar hopes to attend the Clinical Herbalist program in the future. Taylar, aka Sōhka, has been establishing herself as a strong Indigenous female R&B/hip-hop artist over the past year. Taylar comes from a spoken word background, and brings a tremendous sense of strength and wisdom to her writing.

Start the video of Taylar Belanger's interview with Fireside Chats. In the video, Taylar Belanger talks about her journey as a traditional herbalist and how self-expression and music have been a healing experience for her. Taylar talks about the word "protector" and how important the meaning is to her. Taylar's first debut self-produced song is by the same name.

To debrief the video, ask the class the following questions:
1. What are some outlets that helped Taylar get through her personal obstacles?
2. Where does Taylar draw inspiration from?
3. As a traditional herbalist, what do you think a day in her life is like?
4. What does the word protector mean to you?

In Taylar's interview, she talks about how Elders and Healers told her that she is meant to work with Mother Earth and medicines. Inform students that you will be comparing different viewpoints today - western science knowledge and Traditional Ecological Knowledge (TEK).

APPLY: WESTERN SCIENCE AND TRADITIONAL KNOWLEDGES RESEARCH ESSAY

*** Teachers may want to invite an Elder or traditional knowledge keeper to the classroom to talk about the traditional ecological viewpoint first hand.**

Students will write a research essay analyzing the differences and similarities between western science and traditional ecological knowledge. Students will be shown a photo of a field of Fireweed wildflowers. Students will write their essays about what a botanist would see and how they may use the flowers. Then they will research what a traditional medicine person would see and how they may use the flowers. Lastly, they will compare the two worldviews' by analyzing the differences and similarities.

Students will write a 500-word (1-2 page) essay comparing the two worldviews. The essays must include the following:

1. Introduction
2. Western science worldview on ecological knowledge (How would the botanist view a field of flowers? What do they see? What knowledge do they learn from the flowers? How would they use the flowers?)
3. Traditional Indigenous worldview on ecological knowledge (How would the traditional medicine keeper view a field of flowers? What do they see? What knowledge do they learn from the flowers? How would they use the flowers?)
4. How are the two worldviews different? How are they similar?
5. Conclusion
6. Works Cited Page. *You may want to go through with students how to construct a research paper Works Cited Page.*

For the students' research essays, they can use the internet, books, journal articles, talking with traditional knowledge keepers, or talking with an Elder. Students can either be assessed with the essay rubric attached at the bottom or the teacher can use any rubric or assessment tool that their students are already familiar with.

ASSESS:

The Small Group Discussion is a form of formative assessment. Teachers will be able to check students' prior knowledge about how humans impact Mother Earth and the importance that different components play in our ecosystems. Teachers can assess group learning, group dynamics, and student communication skills.

The debriefing questions after Taylar's interview with Fireside Chats is a form of formative assessment. Teachers will be able to check what students took away from Taylar's video and make connections to the other parts of the lesson.

The Western Science and Traditional Research Essay is a summative assessment. Students can be assessed through the essay rubric posted below. Using the rubric is optional. The rubric gives the student a mark out of 25 and room for feedback. Teachers may use their own essay assessment tools as well.

TAKE STUDENT LEARNING FURTHER

Activity: Connection to the Land Journal

If students show a keen interest in learning more about traditional medicines or traditional viewpoints of the land, they can make a write-up about the ways that they connect to the land. As a class, you can make sit-spots for each student. A sit spot is a special space where a student can sit apart from one another. Usually students will silently sit for 10-20 minutes. In their sit-spots, students may use the time to think, daydream, journal, record general observations, or use the space to respond to a specific prompt.

For this activity, in their sit-spots, students will start a journal where they will write about their experiences of connecting to the land. This activity can be a one-time experience or as an on-going learning activity. As different seasons come and go, students will experience different emotions, connections, and relationships with the natural world around them.

English

Print off and copy enough for one of the cards set per group. Cut out cards and place each set into one envelope.

Plant	Person
Sun	Deer
Water	Rock
Spider	Eagle
Bear	Cloud

ASPECTS OF ECOSYSTEMS CUT-OUTS

Anishinaabemowin (optional)

Print off and copy enough for one of the cards set per group. Cut out cards and place each set into one envelope.

Gitigaazh	Anishinaabe
Giizis	Waawaashkeshi
Nibi	Asin
Asabikeshiinh	Migizi
Mahkwa	Aanakwad

Image by Ruby Bruce

Introduction:

For this project, you will write a research essay analyzing the differences and similarities between western science and traditional ecological knowledge. You will answer the question *What are the differences and similarities between the western scientific worldview and the traditional Indigenous worldview when looking at a field of flowers?*

You will research what a botanist and a traditional Indigenous medicine person would see when looking at a field of flowers, including but not limited to aspects such as naming plants, plant uses, and dissemination of knowledge. Compare the two worldview differences and similarities.

For your research you may use the internet, books, journal articles, talking with an Indigenous Knowledge Keepers, or talking with an Indigenous Elder.

Requirements:
- 500-700 words (2 pages)
- Introduction
- Examine the western science viewpoint
- Examine the traditional ecological viewpoint
- Compare and contrast the two viewpoints
- Conclusion
- Reference page

Background:

Traditional Ecological Knowledge, also called by other names including Indigenous Knowledge or Native Science, refers to the evolving knowledge that Indigenous peoples have obtained over hundreds and thousands of years through direct contact with the environment and Mother Earth. This knowledge is specific to the location where they live. It includes the relationships between plants, animals, weather, landscapes and Mother Earth. Knowledge is used for daily life, medicine making, hunting, fishing, trapping, agriculture, and forestry. Traditional Ecological Knowledge is handed down through generations by oral storytelling and hands-on learning.

How do you think the two different perspectives would see this field of Fireweed?

Photo by K8 on Unsplash

WESTERN SCIENCE AND TRADITIONAL KNOWLEDGES RESEARCH ESSAY RUBRIC

Criteria	EXEMPLARY (5)	PROFICIENT (3)	NEARING PROFICIENT (2)	NOVICE (0)
Purpose	The writer's central purpose or argument is readily apparent to the reader	The writing has a clear purpose or argument, but may sometimes digress from it	The central purpose or argument is not consistently clear throughout the paper	The purpose or argument is generally unclear
Content	Balanced presentation of relevant and legitimate information that clearly supports a central purpose or argument and shows a thoughtful, in-depth analysis of a significant topic.	Reader gains important insights. Information provides reasonable support for a central purpose or argument and displays evidence of a basic analysis of a significant topic.	Reader gains some insights. Information supports a central purpose or argument at times. Analysis is basic or general.	Reader gains few insights. Central purpose or argument is not clearly identified. Analysis is vague or not evident. Reader is confused or may be misinformed.
Organization	The ideas are arranged logically to support the purpose or argument. They flow smoothly from one to another and are clearly linked to each other. The reader can easily follow the line of reasonIng.	The ideas are arranged logically to support the central purpose or argument. They are usually clearly linked to each other. For the most part, the reader can follow the line of reasoning.	In general, the writing is arranged logically, although occasionally ideas fail to make sense together. The reader is fairly clear about what the writer intends.	The writing is not logically organized. Frequently, ideas fail to make sense together. The reader cannot identify a line of reasoning and loses interest.
Sentence Structure	Sentences are well-phrased and varied in length and structure. There are no fragments or errors. They flow smoothly from one to another. Word choice is accurate.	Sentences are well-phrased and there is some variety in length and structure. The flow from sentence to sentence is generally smooth. Word choice is mostly accurate.	Some sentences are awkwardly constructed so that the reader is occasionally distracted. Sentence flow is developing. Word choice can be strengthened and more accurate.	Errors in sentence structure are frequent enough to be a major distraction to the reader. No flow and frequently distracting grammatical errors.
Proof of Revision	The writing is free or nearly free of errors.	There are occasional errors, but they don't represent a major distraction or obscure meaning.	The writing has many errors, and the reader is distracted by them.	There are so many errors that the meaning is obscured. The reader is confused and stops reading.

Image by Ruby Bruce

Worldview:

A comprehension viewpoint or philosophy of life, the world, and the universe.

Generally, all worldviews contain a distinct set of beliefs and values that:

- Connection to ancestry and traditional lands
- Establishes identity
- Instill a sense of belonging to a group or place

Indigenous Worldview:

Indigenous nations - for example the Anishinaabe - people believe that all things are interconnected and interrelated. Everything is part of a single whole on Mother Earth. Everything is connected in some way. Anishinaabe people use oral tradition to keep their worldview intact. Oral tradition passes on Anishinaabe worldviews from generation to generation. Oral tradition has always been an integral part of the culture and traditions. Passing knowledge and beliefs from generation to generation serves to maintain the identity and traditions of the community. Indigenous worldviews evolved out of a direct holistic relationship that encompasses one's spirit with every other living thing on Mother Earth. In the Anishinaabe worldview of relationships, there is a deep understanding of respect for self, other people, all animals, and all of nature. Respect for the land and the water is vital. The worldview of Anishinaabe societies is derived from the belief about living together in harmony with nature.

Traditional Ecological Knowledge:

Traditional Ecological Knowledge, also called by other names including Indigenous Knowledge or Native Science, refers to the evolving knowledge that Indigenous peoples have obtained over hundreds and thousands of years through direct contact with the environment and Mother Earth. This knowledge is specific to the location where they live. It includes the relationships between plants, animals, weather, landscapes and Mother Earth. Knowledge is used for daily life, medicine making, hunting, fishing, trapping, agriculture, and forestry. Traditional Ecological Knowledge is handed down through generations by oral storytelling and hands-on learning. Traditional Ecological Knowledge encompasses the worldview of Indigenous people which includes ecology, spirituality, human and animal relationships, and more.

Lesson Two: Pihêsiw Crane

Activity: Healthy Self Analysis

CURRICULUM CONNECTIONS	**Alberta, Northwest Territories & Nunavut:** • Aboriginal Studies Grades 10-12 • English Language Arts Grades 10-12 • English Language Arts Grades 10, 11, 12: Uqausiliriniq Strand • Health and Life Skills Grade 9 • Science Grade 10 **British Columbia and Yukon:** • Contemporary Indigenous Studies Grade 12 • English Language Arts Composition Grades 10, 11, 12 • English Language Arts First Peoples Grade 12 • Physical and Health Education Grade 10 **Ontario:** • English Language Arts Grades 9-10 • English Language Arts Grades 11-12 • First Nations, Metis, and Inuit Studies Grades 9-12 • Health and Physical Education Grades 9-12 • Personal Life Management Grade 12 • Dynamics of Human Relationships Grade 11 • Exploring Family Studies Grades 9-10
DURATION	1 hour
OVERVIEW	In this lesson, students will explore the topics of healthy relationships, healthy self, and sexual and reproductive health careers. Students will begin the lesson discussing what healthy relationships are, how we can keep ourselves healthy in a relationship, and different ways we can keep ourselves healthy aside from the usual physical/fitness health tips. Students will then watch Pihêsiw Crane's interview with Fireside Chats. Using the knowledge learned in Pihêsiw's interview, students will perform an analysis of their own health, plus an analysis of a significant relationship. Students will use a Medicine Wheel graphic organizer to outline ways they keep their emotional, mental, physical, and spiritual selves healthy. Finally, students will analyze their own relationships through a series of self-reflection questions.
MATERIALS	• "Healthy Self, Healthy Relationship Analysis" Worksheets • Whiteboard and markers • Computer, Internet and Projector

Lesson Plan

☀ ACTIVATE: TURN AND TALK ABOUT HEALTHY RELATIONSHIPS

To begin the lesson, pose three different questions to the class. Instruct students to turn to a partner to discuss for 1-2 minutes. Have pairs summarize what they discussed with the rest of the class.

Questions:

1. What does a healthy relationship look like?
2. How can we keep ourselves healthy in a relationship?
3. Are there different ways to keep ourselves healthy besides taking care of our physical bodies?

The discussion questions will activate students' minds into thinking about keeping themselves healthy, and how to keep their relationships (platonic or romantic) healthy.

ACQUIRE: PIHÊSIW CRANE'S FIRESIDE CHAT VIDEO

Pihêsiw Crane (they/them) is from Maskwacis Samson Cree Nation and currently residing in Edmonton, Treaty 6 Territory. They are a queer disabled Nehiyaw who's life work includes Full spectrum Indigenous birthwork, sexual & reproductive health education and land defence activism and water protection. Pishew works with various parts of sexual and reproductive health. As a Full Spectrum Indigenous Birthworker, they support with miscarriage, abortion, adoption, and surrogacy. They work with LGTBQ youth, high-risk youth, and vulnerable populations. Pishew teaches sexual reproductive health through an organization called Native Youth Sexual Healing Network (NYSHN). They also work with the Indigenous Birth of Alberta.

Start the video of Pihêsiw Cranes's interview with Fireside Chats. In the video, Pihêsiw Crane talks about their job working as a Full Spectrum Indigenous Birthworker and sexual and reproductive health educator. A Full Spectrum Indigenous Birthworker is also called a Doula in colonial terms. As a Full Spectrum Indigenous Birthworker, they support with miscarriage, abortion, adoption, and surrogacy.

To debrief the video, ask the class the following questions:

1. What are the many different jobs that Pihêsiw does in the realm of Sexual and Reproductive Health?
2. Why is Indigenous birthwork important?
3. Why does Pihêsiw say they love the work they do?

APPLY: HEALTHY SELF/HEALTHY RELATIONSHIPS ANALYSIS

Students will use their ideas from the activating activity as well as their new knowledge from Pihêsiw's interview to conduct a relationship analysis. Students will examine their own health using a Medicine Wheel graphic organizer.

First, on the Medicine Wheel graphic organizer students will explore their level of health through the four parts of the self. The four parts of the self - according to Anishinaabe (and other Indigenous nations)- are physical, mental, emotional, and spiritual. The physical part of ourselves refers to our physical bodies. Our emotional part of ourselves refers to our emotions, feelings and relationships. The mental part of ourselves refers to our intellect and mental health. The spiritual part of ourselves refers to our spirituality, religion (if applicable) and soul. According to the Anishinaabe worldview, each part of our being is interconnected. We need to make sure that each is healthy so that we are in balance. For example, sometimes when we are emotional and crying, we may get a stomach-ache or a headache. This shows that our emotions are connected to our physical being. To feel better we may smudge, pray, or meditate (spiritual). All of these aspects are interconnected and affect one another. Students will explore this concept and analyze how they keep each part of themselves healthy.

For example, in the physical quadrant, they might write something like "I keep my body healthy by exercising and eating right". In the mental quadrant, they might write something like "I keep my mind healthy by completing my schoolwork as well as learning about mental health". In the emotional category they might write something like "I keep my emotions healthy by writing in a gratitude journal every day". Finally, the spiritual quadrant is the most difficult to explain, as spirit means different things to different people. An example is "I keep my spirit healthy by attending ceremony".

Next, teachers will want to discuss with students the following topics. Make sure to write plenty of examples on the board for students to use later when they complete their own analysis.

1. What does healthy communication look like? Sound like? Feel like?
2. What does unhealthy communication look like? Sound like? Feel like?

3. What are some healthy ways to deal with conflict in a relationship?
4. What are some unhealthy ways to deal with conflict in a relationship?
5. What are boundaries? How do boundaries protect us? How do boundaries protect our relationships?
6. What are some examples of healthy boundaries we can have with people?
7. How do we demonstrate respect in our relationships? How do we know when we are being respected back?

Finally, students will choose one significant relationship in their life and analyze it through a series of self-reflection questions found on the "Relationship Analysis" worksheet.

ASSESS:

The Turn and Talk is a form of formative assessment. Teachers will be able to check students' prior knowledge about what is a healthy relationship, how we can keep ourselves healthy in a relationship, and if there are different ways to be healthy - other than physical health. Teachers can assess group learning, group dynamics, and student communication skills.

The debriefing questions after Pihêsiw's interview with Fireside Chats is a form of formative assessment. Teachers will be able to check what students took away from Pihêsiw's video and make connections to the other parts of the lesson.

The Healthy Self/Healthy Relationships Analysis is a summative assessment. Students will be assessed through how they examine themselves on their worksheets, and through self-reflection questions at the end. Students will be given a mark out of 18.

TAKE STUDENT LEARNING FURTHER

Activity: Sexual Health Toolkit Exploration
Pihêsiw Crane works for an organization called the Native Youth Sexual Healing Network (NYSHN). The Native Youth Sexual Health Network (NYSHN) is an organization by and for Indigenous youth that works across issues of sexual and reproductive health, rights and justice throughout the United States and Canada. NYSHN has a First Nations Sexual Health Toolkit on their website. The learning in the toolkit applies to Indigenous and Non-Indigenous students. In this activity, students can read through both parts of the First Nations Sexual Health Toolkit and explore the various terms, definitions, and sections. Students can then use the information they have learned to create a pamphlet, infographic, or hand-out.

http://www.nativeyouthsexualhealth.com/toolkit.html

Healthy Self, Healthy Relationships Analysis

Overview:

Through this assignment, you are going to analyze yourself in terms of holistic health, including a balanced lifestyle then analyze a significant relationships to see if it is are healthy, unhealthy, or toxic.

For yourself, you will use the Medicine Wheel's four aspects of being to analyze how you are keeping your physical, mental, emotional, and spiritual selves healthy. The four parts of the self - according to Anishinaabe (and other Indigenous nations)- are physical, mental, emotional, and spiritual. The physical part of ourselves refers to our physical bodies. Our emotional part of ourselves refers to our emotions, feelings and relationships. The mental part of ourselves refers to our intellect and mental health. The spiritual part of ourselves refers to our spirituality, religion (if applicable) and soul. All these parts are interconnected. We need to make sure that each part is healthy so that we are in balance. For example, sometimes when someone is so emotional and crying you may get a stomach-ache or a headache. This shows our emotional being is connected to our physical being.

Next, you will choose one significant relationship in your life. You will answer a few self-reflection questions to examine how healthy your relationship currently is. And what you can do to make sure it is, or stays, healthy. Healthy relationships involve respect, communication, kindness, and trust. Relationships can all look different, but healthy relationships have a few things in common such as: open communication, mutual respect, healthy conflict resolution skills and clear, healthy boundaries. You will explore how these concepts align with your own relationships. Relationships, whether platonic or romantic, are very important parts of everyday life. You are going to meet hundreds of people in your lifetime. You will need to know how to keep your relationships stable and healthy!

How do you keep each part of yourself healthy?

Write out **five** strategies you use to keep yourself healthy in each quadrant. On the next page, analyze how each part - Spiritual, Physical, Mental and Emotional - connects to one another. If you run out of room, use a separate piece of paper. *Example: When I am anxious I start to cry and have a stomach ache. My mind is affected by my emotions and physical body. To help, I like to meditate. I use my spirit to bring myself back into balance.*

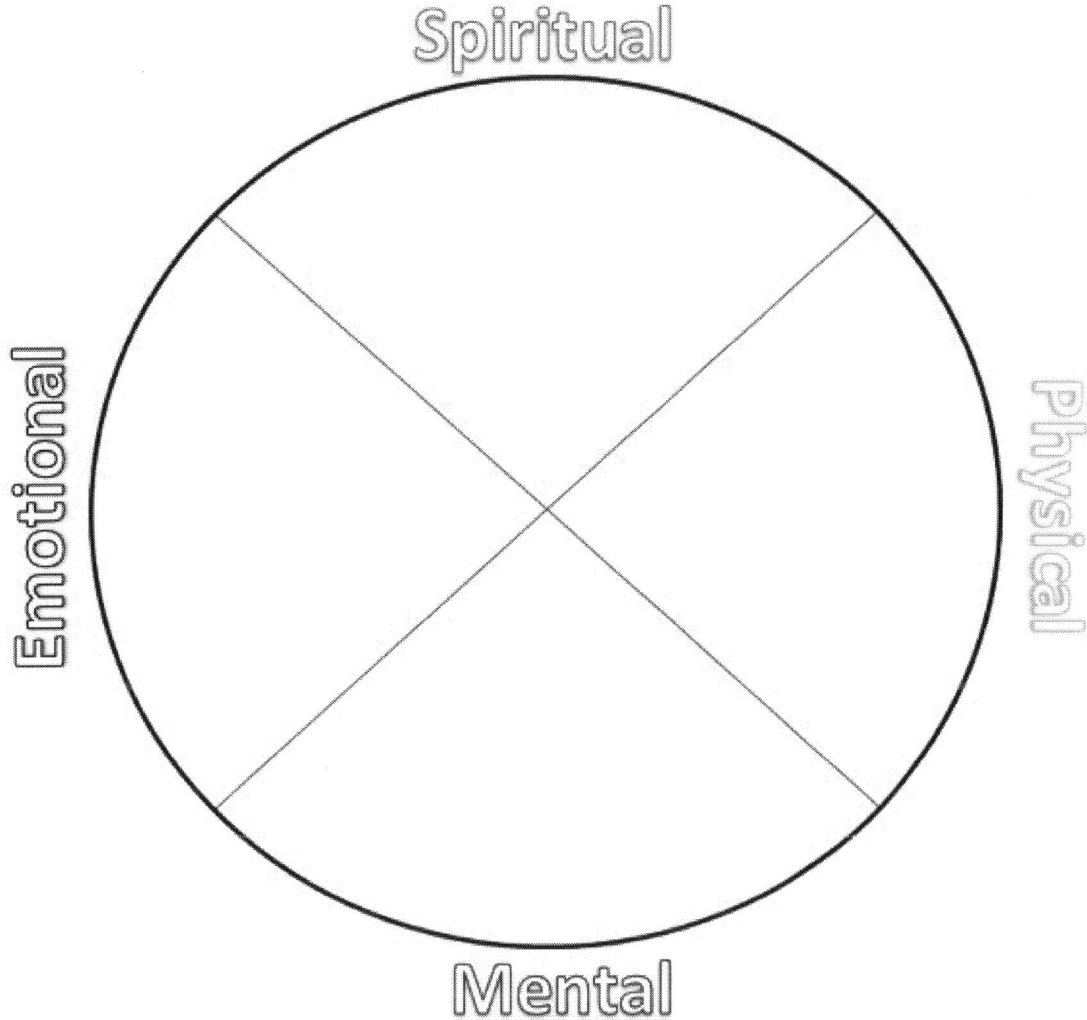

Spiritual

Emotional

Physical

Mental

_____

_____

_____

_____

_____

_____

_____

_____

Are your relationships healthy, unhealthy, or toxic?

Healthy relationships involve boundaries, communication, resolving conflict and respect. All relationships exist on a spectrum, from healthy to toxic to somewhere in between. Choose one significant relationship in your life that you would like to analyze. Then using the Medicine Wheel Aspects of Being, write **two** strategies in each quadrant describing how you will work towards developing or keeping that relationship healthy.

You will examine the relationship of your choice in terms of:

1. How well do we communicate?

Communication is a key part of building and keeping a healthy relationship. The first step in communication is making sure both people want and expect the same things out of the relationship. Even in friendship we need to communicate!

2. How well do we resolve conflict? What strategies do we use to resolve conflict?

Resolving conflict in a relationship can be tough. Fighting, arguing and hitting are not healthy ways to come to a healthy conclusion to a conflict. To resolve conflict both parties need communication, listening skills, clear boundaries, and mutual respect.

3. Are the boundaries in our relationship clear? Healthy?

All healthy relationships require space. Creating clear, healthy boundaries is a great way to keep up your relationship. An example of a boundary is "I will take some space to myself at times"

4. Do I respect this person? Do they respect me?

In what ways do we show that we respect each other? What does respect look like in our relationship?

Persons Name/Alias: _____   Relationship Type: _____

(You can put a fake name/alias for this person if that makes you more comfortable

1. How well do we communicate?

_____

_____

_____

_____

_____

2. How well do we resolve conflict? What strategies do we use to resolve conflict?

_____

_____

_____

_____

_____

3. Are the boundaries in our relationship clear? Healthy? What are they?

_____

_____

_____

_____

_____

4. Do I respect this person? Do they respect me? How do we show it?

_____

_____

_____

_____

_____

5. Is this relationship healthy, unhealth or toxic?

_____

_____

_____

_____

_____

6. Do I need to make any changes in this relationship? How so? How will I know if it is time to walk away from this relationship?

_____

_____

_____

_____

_____

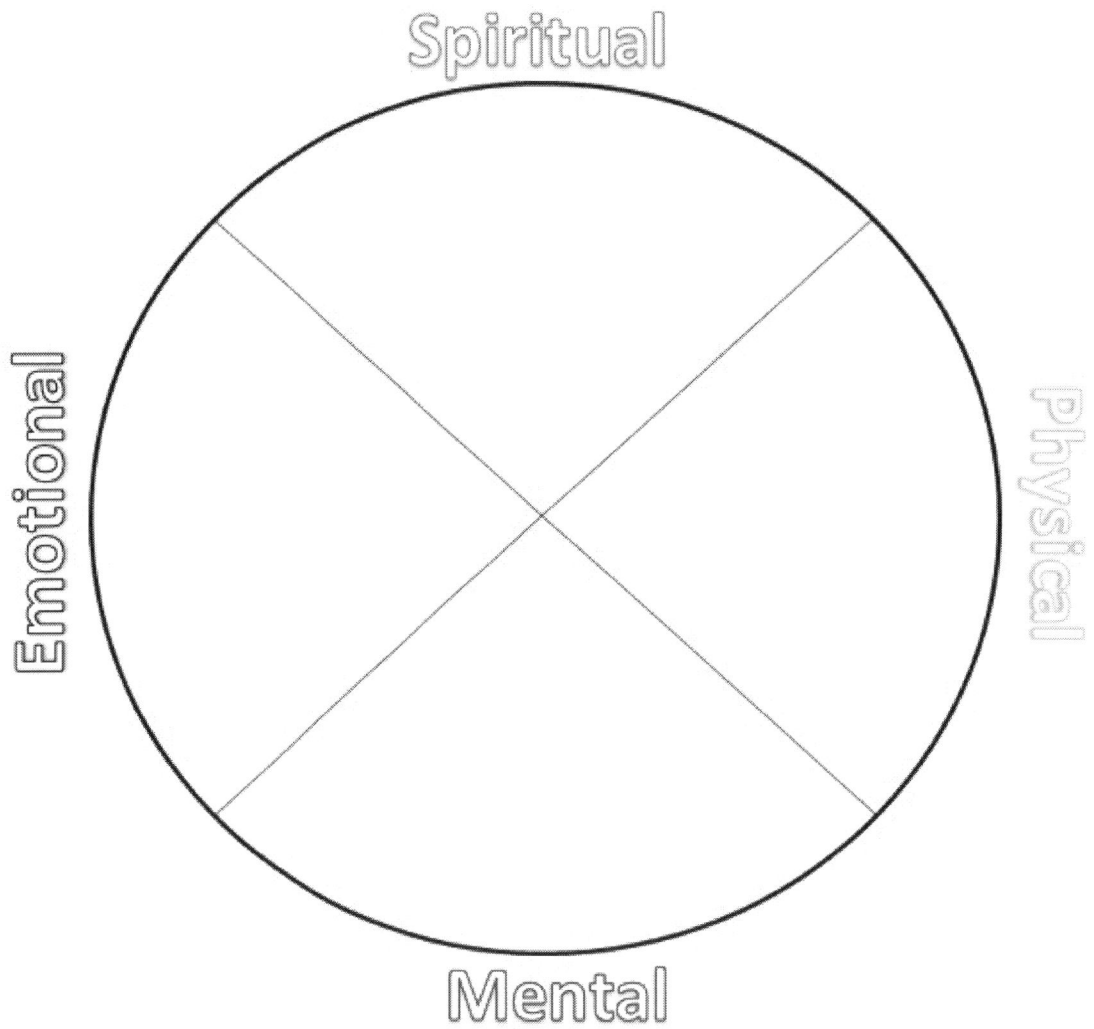

Lesson Three: James Harper

Activity: Community Mapping Project

CURRICULUM CONNECTIONS	**Alberta, Northwest Territories & Nunavut:**

- Aboriginal Studies Grades 10-12
- Biology Grades 11 and 12
- Environmental and Outdoor Education Grade 9
- Geography Grades 11-12
- Science Grade 10
- Science Grades 11 and 12
- Science Grades 10, 11, 12: Iqqaqqaukkaringniq Strand
- Social Studies Grades 10, 20, 30: Nunavusiutit Strand

British Columbia and Yukon:

- Contemporary Indigenous Studies Grade 12
- Earth Sciences Grade 11
- Environmental Science Grade 11
- Environmental Science Grade 12

Ontario:

- First Nations, Metis, and Inuit Studies Grades 9-12
- Biology Grades 9-12
- Earth Sciences Grades 9-10
- Scientific Investigation Skills and Career Exploration Grades 9-12
- Environmental Science Grade 11

DURATION	2-3+ hours

OVERVIEW	In this lesson, students will explore the topics of sustainability, clean energy, relationships to the land and Mother Earth, impacts of protecting our communities and careers that protect our land. Students will consider careers that impact Mother Earth and help ensure sustainability for future generations. As a class, students will discuss different careers working directly with Mother Earth and what the impacts might be. Students will watch James Harper's Fireside Chat interview where James talks about his journey becoming an engineer working in the clean energy sector. James talks about his passion of clean energy and bringing the engineering discipline to the forefront to create sustainability for our seven generations ahead. James discusses the knowledge he has gained from Elders and his reconnection to the land. Students will then investigate their own communities and ways that Mother Earth is protected, sustained, and cared for, by participating in a community walk. After examining their community, students will create individual community maps outlining infrastructure, water resources, parks, community resources and more. Students will be assessed by peer-assessment using a checklist and feedback form.

MATERIALS	

- Clipboards
- Writing instruments (pencil, pens)
- Large white paper
- Rulers
- Colouring instruments (pencil crayons, markers, permanent markers)
- "Community Mapping Project" handout

ACTIVATE: CLASS DISCUSSION

To begin the lesson, hold a whole class discussion on different careers people may have where they work directly with Mother Earth.

Ask Students the Following Questions:

1. What are some careers where a person works directly with Mother Earth?
Example: Think of jobs outdoors, in parks, at zoos, construction/infrastructure, with plants or animals, etc...

2. What are some negative impacts that some jobs/careers could have on Mother Earth?
Example: Deforestation removes trees and ruins habitats. Road construction upheaves the land and puts down cement.

3. What are some positive impacts that some jobs/careers could have on Mother Earth?
Example: National Park Conservationists remove invasive species and replant trees. Engineers find clean energy sources to sustain Mother Earth. Some zoos help with repopulating endangered species.

Use the last discussion question as a segway into talking about James Harper and his career as an engineer working in the clean energy sector.

ACQUIRE: JAMES HARPER'S FIRESIDE CHAT VIDEO

https://www.firesidechats.ca/video/james-harper

James Harper, also known as Mihskakwan (Red Cloud), is a Nihiyaw man from Sturgeon Lake Cree Nation on Treaty 8 Territory. He was born in Edmonton, Alberta and grew up in Winnipeg, Manitoba. James completed a Bachelor of Science in Mechanical Engineering at the University of Manitoba and is currently working on a Masters degree in Renewable Energy. James has been studying overseas in places such as Barcelona, Stockholm, and Paris, to study more about the integration of renewable energy in our energy sources of tomorrow. James' passion for clean energy has naturally evolved over time. He wants to carry forth the promise his ancestors had to protect the Earth and future generations. James is also a conference organizer for Seven Gen, an Indigenous Youth conference that brings awareness to youth across Canada about understanding their inner strength and empowers them to believe they can make a difference in their own communities and on a bigger scale.

Show the class the video of James Harper's interview with Fireside Chats or have them read the textbook chapter. In the video, James Harper talks about his job working as an engineer. James describes his fundamental roots as a Cree man is understanding what his ancestors have envisioned for the next seven generations ahead. Which is a clean, protected Earth. He describes this as the true definition of sustainability. James as a passion for clean energy and wants to bring sustainability to our future generations.

To debrief the video, ask the class the following questions:

1. Why is James passionate about the clean energy sector and land sustainability?
2. Why do you think James said the land is one of the greatest teachers out there?
3. What does James describe as the true definition of sustainability?

In James' interview he talks about having a sustainable environment and protecting our lands. Students will use this new knowledge to map their communities and to look out for ways sustainability is happening in their home communities as well as opportunities for improvement.

***We encourage you to invite Indigenous Elders or Knowledge Keepers to your classroom to help plan the walk, and give teachings on the land in that area.**

Students will investigate their own community for ways that Mother Earth is protected, sustained, and cared for, by participating in a community walk. Students will walk around their community and create individual community maps outlining infrastructure, water resources, parks, community resources and more. Students will explore what resources in their community protect Mother Earth, and what issues there may be that might harm the environment. Using this information, students will brainstorm ways their community can become more sustainable in the future.

Handout and review the "Community Mapping Project" handout with students. Go over the assignment expectations as well as the reflection questions on the back.

Go on a walk with your students! Students may need to walk more than once while creating their maps. In respect to land based education, getting the students outside as much as possible with this assignment is strongly encouraged!

Teacher Tip: Before doing a community walk, you should be clear about your expectations so students don't stray away from the purpose of the walk. It's a fun experience but it is also very easy for students to get distracted. To do this, you might want to give students examples of behaviours that are acceptable, and behaviours that are unacceptable. See #3 for specific examples.

Community Walk Preparation Steps:
1. Set a clear purpose for the walk.
The purpose of this community walk is to find how well our community is protecting Mother Earth. You will be looking for resources/infrastructure that help protect the environment as well as issues that you see in the community that could hurt the Earth.

2. Pose a learning question for the students to consider.
How is our community protecting Mother Earth? How is our community hurting Mother Earth?

3. Create clear expectations for the walk.
On this walk we will be walking on the sidewalk. We will not be stepping on people's private property. We may invite Elders, Knowledge Keepers, other school staff etc. We will be walking for x amount of minutes.

4. Create a route beforehand
Either on your own or with your students.

Land-Based Education: Why is it important?
Being and learning outside provides so many benefits. There is a lot that anyone can learn from the land that are not just wilderness survival skills. We can use the Earth to connect back to ourselves and to promote self-growth. From the Anishinaabe perspective, the people have a profound spiritual and physical connection to the land. Many Anishinaabe people consider the land and Mother Earth to be a part of their identity. We see this through the teachings that the land provides us and the ones you can apply to ourselves and our lives. Anishinaabe people believe the land is the main and most sacred tool for education. Many parts of the environment and Earth can provide us with important teachings. As well, being outside and having access to nature can help reduce stress, provide appreciation for nature, and so much more!

Upon return from the community walk, lead a class discussion.
Ask Students:
1. What did you notice about our community?
2. What was your reaction to seeing it? Surprised? Angry? Encouraged?
3. What issue(s) do you think there are?
4. What community resources are in place to help with this issue?
5. Are those resources enough? What more can we, or the community, do?

ASSESS:

The class discussions are a form of formative assessment. Teachers will be able to check students' prior knowledge about what careers they think relate to Mother Earth, how some jobs can negatively impact Earth, and how some jobs can positively impact Earth. Teachers can assess group learning and student communication skills.

The debriefing questions after James' interview with Fireside Chats is a form of formative assessment. Teachers will be able to check what students took away from James' video and make connections to the other parts of the lesson.

The Community Mapping Project is a summative assessment. Students will be assessed through peer assessment and teacher feedback. For their maps, teachers may use their own rubrics or assessment tools.

TAKE STUDENT LEARNING FURTHER

Activity: Clean Energy and Sustainability Awareness Campaign Project
If students show a keen interest in learning more about what clean energy is and how they can lead more sustainable lives; students can create a Clean Energy and Sustainability Awareness campaign. Students would research different ways clean energy positively impacts our society and environment. With their research, they can make posters and go on a parade walk through the school or community to showcase their learning.

Overview

You will investigate our community around the school to see if Mother Earth is being protected, sustained, and cared for. To do this you will be going on a **community walk**! A community walk is where you walk around where you live or where you go to school.

After examining the community, you will create an individual **Community Map**. The map will outline infrastructure, water resources, parks, community resources and more. You will explore what resources in your community protect Mother Earth. As well as what resources in your community might harm Mother Earth. After creating the community map, you will answer the **Community Evaluation Questions** below. Answer the questions on a separate piece of paper.

Community Mapping:

Create a Community Map of your community. You may need to walk around a few times. It's great to bring a clipboard to write or draw as you walk.

On your map you will:

1. Include 20-30 different infrastructure, water resources, community resources, etc. *Example: Houses, public buildings, schools, stores, trees, bodies of water, pools, garbage cans, recycling bins.*
2. Make a **map key** and colour code each aspect. *Example: Houses are coloured green. Water is coloured blue. Etc.*
3. Include street and road names.

Example of a Community Map:

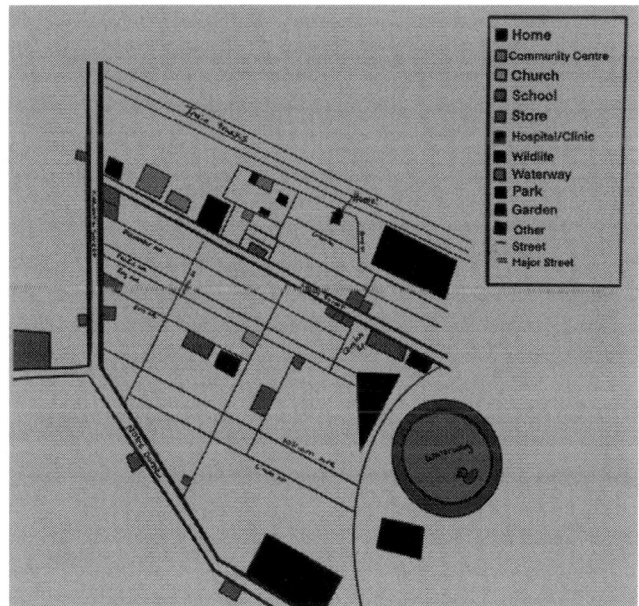

Community Evaluation Question Sheet

Answer the following questions on a separate sheet of paper. Write 5-8 sentences for each question.

1. What did you notice about things that are helping to protect the environment in your community?
2. What did you see that might be a sign of an issue in your community?
3. What are some actions you're, or your community, are already taking to protect the environment?
4. What are three things you would want to add to your community to make it more eco-friendly and better protect Mother Earth?

Lesson One: Evan Redsky
Activity: Storytelling Through Song

CURRICULUM CONNECTIONS	**Alberta, Northwest Territories and Nunavut:** • Aboriginal Studies Grades 10-12 • English Language Arts Grades 10-12 • English Language Arts Grades 10, 11, 12: Uqausiliriniq Strand • General Music Grades 10-12: **British Columbia and Yukon:** • Contemporary Indigenous Studies Grade 12 • Contemporary Music Grades 10, 11, 12 • English Language Arts Composition Grades 10, 11, 12 • English Language Arts First Peoples Grade 12 **Ontario:** • First Nations, Metis, and Inuit Studies Grades 9-12 • English Language Arts Grades 9-10 • English Language Arts Grades 11-12 • Music Grades 9-10 • Music Grade 11, University/College Preparation • Music Grade 12, University/College Preparation
DURATION	2-3 hours
OVERVIEW	In this lesson, students will explore the topics of artistic expression, resilience, music, and storytelling. Students will participate in a class poll where they will talk about their favourite songs. Songs hold many meanings, themes, and stories within them. Oral tradition and Storytelling was, and still is, the epitome of learning in all Indigenous cultures. In Red River Metis and Anishinaabe culture, families pass down their histories, traditions, and experiences through oral tradition. Oral tradition is an intergenerational transmission of knowledge, teachings and spirituality. We suggest having an Elder or traditional knowledge keeper visit your class to give a teaching on storytelling and oral tradition. Students will watch Evan Redsky's interview with Fireside Chats. Evan Redsky is an Indigenous singer/songwriter with a love of storytelling from a young age. Evan has been a musician for over a decade and recently decided to work on a solo career. Students will create song lyrics that tell a short story. The theme of their songs will reflect a time in their life they had to overcome an obstacle. This activity is not a full introduction to songwriting. This activity will have students making connections between storytelling and music while conveying the theme of their song. Students will create a song with 3 verses and a chorus. Songs must have flow and rhythm. Students will be assessed by a writing assessment rubric.
MATERIALS	• Computer Access for each students • "Storytelling Through Song" Handout • "Writing Assessment" Rubric • Writing Instruments (pencils, pens, etc) and Lined paper

ACTIVATE: YOUR FAVOURITE SONG POLL

To begin the lesson, play your favourite song for the class! You can have students try to guess why they are listening to music today. After a few guesses, instruct them that today you will be learning about storytelling through song. Ask students "what is your favourite song?". Pause and let students think to themselves for about 30 seconds. Go around the class and have students say their favourite songs out loud. Remind students to stay respectful and thoughtful with their answers. Write out the list on the board. If a song appears more than once, put a checkmark or star next to it.

Ask the question "Do any of these songs tell a story?" Listen to students' rationale and answers about if any of the songs tell a story. Instruct them that many songs are meant to tell stories and that there are whole albums out there dedicated to telling one single story through multiple songs. Today, as a class, you will be looking into the journey of Evan Redsky, an Indigenous singer/songwriter who likes to tell stories through his music.

Extension:

At the end, you will have a long list of songs that you could create into a class playlist (without explicit content). You can save the playlist to listen to while students are working, or as a greeting to start the morning/class!

ACQUIRE: EVAN REDSKY'S FIRESIDE CHAT VIDEO

Evan Redsky is an Anishinaabe singer/songwriter from Mississaugi First Nation, Blind River, Ontario located north of Toronto. Evan has been working in the music industry for over ten years. Evan has played and toured with rock bands, and then recently has been dedicated to his solo career as a singer/songwriter. Evan grew up with a love of storytelling that manifested itself through both music and performance. From a young age he was constantly writing songs and appearing in plays. While he left home as a teenager to pursue classical acting at Fanshawe College, he still maintained ties with his community, appreciative of his Indigenous roots and the deep history behind them.

Start the video of Evan Redsky's interview with Fireside Chats. In the interview, Evan discusses his career and journey as an Indigenous musician and singer/songwriter. Evan explores his journey to become a singer/songwriter while highlighting some of his obstacles that stood in his way.

To debrief the video, ask the class the following questions:

1. What inspired Evan to become a singer/songwriter?
2. What were some lessons/obstacles that Evan faced on his career journey?
3. What advice does Evan give to young Indigenous people who are about to leave their home communities?

Students will use the teachings from Evan's interview with Fireside Chats to create their own story through song lyrics.

APPLY: STORYTELLING THROUGH SONG

** We suggest having an Elder or traditional knowledge keeper visit your class to give a teaching about storytelling and oral tradition.

Students will create song lyrics that tell a short story about a time in their life they had to overcome an obstacle/barrier. Students will create 3 verses and a chorus that separates the verses. This activity is not a full introduction to songwriting. However, this activity will have students making connections between storytelling and music.

Storytelling is important in Red River Metis and Anishinaabe cultures for sharing knowledge, traditions and morals. Many stories in Red River Metis and Anishinaabe cultures hold a variety of meanings. The same story may be told at different points in a person's life; for when they need a new meaning. Students will consider this information while creating their song lyrics. Songs must have flow, rhythm and follow the theme of overcoming obstacles and resiliency.

Handout the "Storytelling through Song" handout. Read the introduction and instructions with the class. Instruct students to use the storyboard to write out ideas for each of their verses and chorus. Students will be provided with a small checklist they can refer to while creating their lyrics. Students will make one rough draft and one final copy.

With their rough draft, students will peer edit each other's drafts. Students will refer to the song lyric checklist, and edit for flow, rhythm, clarity, spelling, and grammar.

After receiving their rough drafts back, students can type out their final copies. Final copies will be handed in and marked.

ASSESS:

The classroom poll list of students' favourite songs is a form of formative assessment. This activity is to activate students' minds and get the class thinking about music. Teachers can check student thinking, and assess their communication skills.

The debriefing questions after Evan's interview with Fireside Chats is a form of formative assessment. Teachers will be able to check what students took away from Raven's video and make connections to the other parts of the lesson.

The Storytelling Through Song assignment is a summative assessment. Students will be assessed through a writing assessment rubric.

TAKE STUDENT LEARNING FURTHER

Activity: Song Analysis Project

To take students' learning further, students can complete a project analyzing one of their favourite song's themes, meanings, and stories that the artist is trying to convey. Students can take a song that holds meaning to them and compare the message of what the artist was conveying, to the meaning that the song holds to them. Students could make posters, videos, multimedia presentations, etc. about their research findings. At the end, the class could do a walk-through and view each other's projects.

STORYTELLING THROUGH SONG

Introduction:
Storytelling is an oral tradition used by many cultures all over the world. In Indigenous cultures, such as Red River Metis and Anishinaabe cultures, families pass down their histories, traditions, and experiences through oral tradition. Oral tradition is an intergenerational transmission of knowledge, teachings and spirituality. Usually from Elders to their children to their grandchildren. Songs also tell a story through lyrics and music.

Storytelling Song Lyrics Instructions:
For this assignment, you will tell a story through writing song lyrics. You will tell a story about a time you faced an obstacle/barrier in your life or had a moment of resiliency. Resiliency is recovering from a challenge in your life.

You will need to write out 3 verses and a chorus. A chorus is a part of a song that is repeated after each verse. Each verse needs 4-6 lines of lyrics. To keep the flow, use the same amount of lines in each verse

Image created by Ruby Bruce, Zhaawenoodin.

if possible. Chorus needs 4-6 lines of lyricsThe lyrics will have to flow well together and have some sort of rhythmic pattern. Flow and rhythmic pattern is what makes your lyrics read like a song. Think of it as a beat or even rhyming. In songs words don't have to perfectly rhyme like cat and bat. Your lyrics may loosely rhyme like the words cat and act. The lyrics could mimic a pop song, folk song, rap song, etc. Have fun and be creative!

Storyboard:
Use this organizer to draw or write out your ideas for your verses and chorus.

Verse One	Chorus	Verse Two	Verse Three

Song Lyric Checklist:
Use this checklist to remember what you need to include in your storytelling song lyrics.

- Verse one introduces the story
- Verse one is 4-6 lines long
- Chorus comes after verse one
- Chorus is 4-6 lines long
- Verse two is 4-6 lines long
- Verse three is 4-6 lines long
- Lyrics tell a story about you overcoming an obstacle/barrier or shows you being resilient
- Lyrics flow well together and have a rhythmic pattern
- Story is clear and not confusing
- There are no spelling or grammatical errors

STORYTELLING WRITING ASSESSMENT RUBRIC

Name: _____

CATEGORIES OF PERFORMANCE:	BEGINNER (0)	BASIC (1)	INTERMEDIATE (2)	ADVANCED (3)
Flow and Rhythm	There is no clear flow or rhythmic pattern to the lyrics.	Lyrics do not have a clear rhythmic pattern and do not flow that easily well.	Lyrics flow somewhat well together, and show good rhythmic pattern to the words.	Lyrics flow well together and show that there is a great rhythmic pattern to the words.
Clarity and Organization of ideas	Assignment is not clear and very vague. Assignment is not well organized.	Assignment is somewhat clear. 3+ thoughts are vague and unclear. Organization needs improvement.	Assignment is mostly clear but, 1-2 thoughts are vague. Ideas are mostly organized.	Assignment is well written, clear, and ideas are organized well.
Theme	No representation of the theme of overcoming obstacles and/or resiliency.	Minimal representation of the theme of overcoming obstacles and/or resiliency.	Good representation of the theme of overcoming obstacles and/or resiliency.	The themes of overcoming obstacles and/or resiliency
Time, Effort and Creativity	Writing assignments show that no time or effort was put in. Lacks creativity.	Minimal time and effort were used for creativity for the writing assignment.	Some effort and time were used for the assignment.. Lyrics are creative.	Student went above and beyond with the creativity in their lyrics. Shows great time and effort.
Spelling and grammar	There are many errors in spelling, capitalization, grammar and punctuation.	There are some errors in spelling, capitalization, grammar and punctuation.	There are only a few errors in spelling, capitalization, grammar and punctuation.	There are no errors in spelling, capitalization, grammar or punctuation

/15

Teacher Feedback:

Lesson Two: Dakota Bear
Activity: Mental Well-being Stress Kits

CURRICULUM CONNECTIONS	**Alberta, Northwest Territories and Nunavut:** • Aboriginal Studies Grades 10-12 • English Language Arts Grades 10-12 • English Language Arts Grades 10, 11 and 12: Uqausiliriniq Strand • Health and Life Skills Grade 9 • School Health: Mental and Emotional Well Being Grade 9 • Psychology Grades 11-12 **British Columbia and Yukon:** • Contemporary Indigenous Studies Grade 12 • English Language Arts Composition Grades 10, 11 and 12 • English Language Arts First Peoples Grade 12 • Physical and Health Education Grade 10 • Contemporary Indigenous Studies Grade 12 • English Language Arts Composition Grades 10, 11 and 12 • English Language Arts First Peoples Grade 12 • Physical and Health Education Grade 10 **Ontario:** • First Nations, Metis, and Inuit Studies Grades 9-12 • English Language Arts Grades 9-10 • English Language Arts Grades 11-12 • Introduction to Anthropology, Psychology, and Sociology Grade 11 • Health and Physical Education Grades 9-12 • Personal Life Management
DURATION	1-2 hours
OVERVIEW	In this lesson, students will explore the topics of mental health, social justice issues, and stepping out of their comfort zones. Students will listen to Indigenous hip-hop artist Dakota Bear's song "Freedom". While listening to the song, students will write down keywords from the video and feelings/emotions that the song evokes. Students will watch Dakota Bear's interview with Fireside Chats. Dakota Bear is also an activist for Indigenous social justice movements such as Idle No More and MMIWG2S (Missing and Murdered Indigenous Women, Girls and Two-Spirit). From the teachings in Dakota's video, students will reflect on their own mental wellbeing as they create their own stress kits. Stress kits are an amazing way to develop and apply coping strategies to manage students' own emotions and mental health. Creating stress kits encourages mindfulness and teaches students to recognize the physiological signs of stress on their physical, emotional, mental, and spiritual health. This lesson is great on its own or in conjunction with other lessons about stress, mental wellbeing, and/or keeping all aspects of ourselves healthy. Students self-reflect about their stress kits, their experience, and why taking care of their mental wellbeing is important.
MATERIALS	• One small box or shoebox per student • Computer Access • Access to Youtube, Spotify, Apple Music or Dakota Bear's website • Whiteboard and markers • "Mental Wellbeing Stress Kit" Handout • Stress Kit made by the teacher *(Optional)* • "How-to-Make a Stress Ball" handout *(Optional)* • Materials to make stress balls *(Optional)* • Any other materials teachers want to use for the creation of stress kit items *(Optional)*

✳ ACTIVATE: "FREEDOM" WORD SPLASH

To begin the lesson, tell students that today they will be learning about the career of Dakota Bear, an Indigenous hip-hop artist and activist. Dakota works hard to bring light to issues that surround Indigenous peoples and he also puts mental well-being into the spotlight. As a class, you will listen to Dakota's song "Freedom". As students listen to the song, they will write down keywords, recurring themes, and/or feelings/emotions they have while listening to the song. When the song is finished, as a class you will create a word splash on the whiteboard using the different words and feelings students described.

You may want to listen to the song 2-3 times for students to really understand the message that Dakota is trying to portray. While creating the word splash, the teacher can encourage students to either write down the same word splash, or design their own in their notes.

👥 ACQUIRE: DAKOTA BEAR'S FIRESIDE CHAT VIDEO

https://www.firesidechats.ca/video/dakota-bear

Dakota Bear is a Saskatoon-born, Vancouver-based Indigenous hip-hop artist and activist. His melodic rhymes carry stories of Indigenous peoples across Canada leaving listeners enlightened, inspired and instant fans of his music and message. His performances range from audiences of 30,000 (Global Climate Strike with Greta Thunberg, Downtown Vancouver, October 2019) to inspirational performances for youth in remote communities in Northern Canada. His work with Idle No More, Missing and Murdered Indigenous Women, Girls and Two-Spirited Peoples and the Global Climate Strike movement has intertwined his music with international social justice movements and connected him with fans across the country. He's shared stages with legendary greats like Bone Thugs n Harmony, Redman & Methodman, TechN9ne and more.

Show the video of Dakota Bear's interview with Fireside Chats.

To debrief the video, ask the class the following questions:

1. What does Dakota mean when he calls himself a "Warrior Entrepreneur"?
2. Why is it important to try new things and step out of our comfort zone?
3. What is intergenerational trauma? How does it relate to mental health?

Inform students that they will use the teachings from Dakota's video and create a stress-kit that they will be able to use in the future to take care of their mental health. Students will use this experience to self-reflect about their own mental wellbeing.

💡 APPLY: MENTAL WELL-BEING STRESS KITS

Hand out the "Mental Well-being Stress Kits" handout. Students will create their own stress kits that will help them when they are feeling stressed, sad, overwhelmed, and need to feel grounded. The kits will help students cope with the stresses in their everyday lives at school and home. Stress kits are an amazing way to develop and apply coping strategies to manage students' physical, emotional, mental, and spiritual wellbeing by focussing on their emotions and mental health. In Anishinaabe culture, each aspect of health is interconnected and affects each other. If one part of ourselves is not well, then our entire self will be thrown out of balance.

Students **must** include at least **six** things for their kits. Some examples of items students could **make**:

- Stress Ball
- Calm Down Jar

- Play dough (lavender or vanilla scented)
- Small crocheted blanket
- Kaleidoscope
- Relaxation prompt cards
- Soothing sounds CD
- Photo album or scrapbook of loved ones
- Handwritten poem
- Letter to self
- Positive Affirmations List

Examples of other items that could be included (*that students could bring from home*):

- Fidget tools/toys (Pop-it, fidget spinner, etc.)
- Colouring book and pencil crayons
- Favourite book
- Fuzzy socks
- Stuffed animal
- Tissues
- Journal and pen/pencil (for writing or doodling)
- Bubbles

These kits will look different for each student! Students can get very creative with their boxes. Once students are finished creating their boxes. They will answer the self-reflection questions at the end of the "Mental Well-Being Stress Kit" handout.

ASSESS:

The word splash about Dakota Bear's song "Freedom" is a form of formative assessment. This activity is to activate students' minds and get the class analyzing their own thoughts. Teachers can check student thinking, and assess their analytical and communication skills.

The debriefing questions after Dakota's interview with Fireside Chats is a form of formative assessment. Teachers will be able to check what students took away from Raven's video and make connections to the other parts of the lesson.

The stress kit and self-reflection question are a summative assessment. Students will assess their own stress kits, their experience making the kits, and reflect on the importance of mental wellbeing.

TAKE STUDENT LEARNING FURTHER

Activity: Your Mental Health Playlist
To take students' learning further, and have them reflect more about their mental wellbeing, students can create their own mental health playlist. In this activity, students choose 10-20 songs that they can play when they are either feeling down, stressed, or overwhelmed and/or songs they can play when they want to feel happy, empowered or to become motivated. Students can make the playlist on a multimedia app or website. Students can reflect on why they chose their songs and play one for the class. Teachers can even take some of the song ideas (ones without explicit content) and make a class playlist to help students feel grounded.

MENTAL WELL-BEING STRESS KITS

Name: _____

Introduction:
Our mental well-being is very important to take care of. Our mental and emotional health impacts us in every way. Stress is something that can negatively impact our mental wellbeing. Understanding your own experiences and learning healthy ways to cope with stress is important. We all need to learn how to recognize when stress is affecting us and ways to properly manage the stress. Stress kits are an amazing way to develop and apply coping strategies to manage our stress so we can feel balanced.

Stress Kits Instructions:
For this activity, you will create a stress kit that you can use for whenever you're feeling overwhelmed, down, sad, angry, or need to feel grounded. Everyone will have different ways they cope with stress. There are many things we can do to help us feel balanced again!

You will use a small box or shoebox as your stress kit. **Decorate** your box as you please. You want it to make you feel happy, calm, or grounded when you see it. You will choose **six** things to include in your stress kit. You will need to make **four** of the items in your stress kit. The other two things can be items you have from home. There are so many things you can choose from, have fun and be creative!

Examples of Items you can make: *(These are just ideas! You may come up with other objects):*

- Stress Ball
- Play dough (lavender or vanilla scented)
- Calm Down Jar
- Crocheted blanket
- Kaleidoscope
- Relaxation prompt cards
- Soothing sounds CD
- Letter to self
- Handwritten poem
- Positive Affirmations List
- Photo album or scrapbook of loved ones

ITEMS/OBJECTS IN YOUR KIT:

1. _____

2. _____

3. _____

4. _____

5. _____

6. _____

SELF-REFLECTION QUESTIONS:

Answer the following questions on a separate sheet of paper. Write 5-8 sentences per question. Write in full sentences and explain your thinking.

1. What four objects did you make? Explain which was the easiest to make and which was the hardest to make.

2. Which two objects did you choose? Explain why you chose them.

3. How will your objects help you cope with stress in your everyday life? Explain how you are going to use each item.

4. Why is taking care of our mental well-being important?

5. Many Indigenous peoples are impacted by intergenerational trauma. How do you think this impacts their mental and emotional health?

Stress balls are excellent sensory tools to help people release stress, become grounded and feel balanced again. Stress balls are easy to create and only need a few simple materials.

Materials:
- One funnel
- One pair of scissors
- Small, round balloon (per person)
- One cup of corn starch or flour (per person)

Instructions:

1. Blow up the balloon.
Blow air into the balloon until it is slightly inflated. To about 3-4 inches in diameter. Do not tie the balloon but, you will need to keep the balloon inflated as best you can.

2. Pinch the balloon closed.
Pinch the top of the balloon shut, leaving room for the funnel to be inserted into the neck of the balloon.

3. Insert the funnel into the balloon.
Place a funnel inside the opening of the balloon while still pinching the balloon closed. You may need help securing the funnel inside the balloon. *Don't worry if your balloon deflates a little, as this may happen during this step.*

4. Fill your balloon.
Fill the top of the funnel with flour or cornstarch. Add your filling until the balloon is filled. *It works best to add a small amount of the flour or cornstarch at a time. If you let too much go in too quickly, then air leaving the balloon will blow flour/cornstarch into the air and make a mess.*

5. Squeeze out the excess air.
Pull up tightly on the opening of the balloon and pinch out any extra air out. In order to have an effective stress ball that won't pop, it's important to eliminate any extra air that's inside your balloon.

6. Tie the balloon closed.
Knot the balloon closed as close to the filling as you can. Use scissors to cut off any excess balloon. Do not cut too close to the knot.

Lesson One: Monique (Mo) Aura Bedard

Activity: Art Therapy

CURRICULUM CONNECTIONS	**Alberta, Northwest Territories and Nunavut:** • Aboriginal Studies Grades 10-12: • Art 10,20,30 • School Health Program **British Columbia and Yukon:** • Contemporary Indigenous Studies Grade 12 • Physical and Health Education Grade 10 **Ontario:** • First Nations, Metis, and Inuit Studies Grades 9-12 • Health and Physical Education Grades 9-12 • Personal Life Management Grade 12 • Dynamics of Human Relationships Grade 11 • Exploring Family Studies Grades 9-10
DURATION	1-2 hours
OVERVIEW	Throughout this lesson, students will participate in a Think/Pair/Share activating activity where they will discuss the concept of coping strategies, including the definition of coping strategies and the difference between healthy and unhealthy strategies. Students will then watch Monique (Mo) Aura Bedard's interview about her journey becoming an Art Therapist and using art as a tool to teach about mental health. Students will take the information learned in the video and apply the concepts to their own lives by engaging in at least one art therapy exercise. Students will self-assess their art based on the rubric posted below.
MATERIALS	• "Art Therapy Activities Menu" handout • Poster Paper (various size options) • Magazines • Scissors • Glue • Paint/Paint Brushes or Pencil Crayons

Lesson Plan

☀ ACTIVATE: COPING STRATEGIES THINK/PAIR/SHARE

Pose the question "What is a coping strategy?" to the class. Instruct students to first think about their answer. Then, have students' pair with a partner and take turns sharing their answers. Once pairs have fully discussed the answer, solicit volunteers to share what they discussed with the whole group.

Coping strategies are things that we can do to help us manage our emotions. When we are angry, sad, annoyed etc. we can do certain things to help us feel better.

Next, ask "What are some examples of healthy coping strategies?" Have students go through the Think/Pair/Share process again. Once pairs have fully discussed the answer, solicit volunteers to share what they discussed with the whole group.

Answers will vary. Examples of healthy coping strategies can include venting to a friend, talking with a therapist, exercising, going for walk, listening to music etc.

Ask students "What are some examples of un-healthy coping strategies?" Have students go through the Think/Pair/Share process again. Once pairs have fully discussed the answer, solicit volunteers to share what they discussed with the whole group.

Answers will vary. Unhealthy coping strategies can be thought of as things that we can do to help us manage are emotions that have the potential to make things worse. Examples can include yelling at people, breaking things, or turning to drugs and alcohol. If every time we are upset, we yell at the people around us, that has the potential to make our lives worse in the long run because it is going to negatively affect our relationships. If every time we are upset, we break things, that has the potential to make our lives worse in the long run because we can hurt ourselves, others and/or damage property that we must pay for. If every time we are sad, we turn to drugs or alcohol to make us feel better, that has the potential to make our lives worse in the long run because we can develop an addiction.

Finally, ask students "why might it be important to have a "toolbox" of healthy coping strategies handy for when we need to use them?"

Answers may vary. It might be important to have a "toolbox" of healthy coping strategies handy for when we need them because unfortunately, negative events are part of life, and we never know when we might need to make ourselves feel better in a healthy way. If we have a healthy plan for when negative things happen, we are more likely to get through it without making things worse.

Inform the class that today we are going to be learning about Monique (Mo) Aura Bedard's journey becoming an Art Therapist.

ACQUIRE: MONIQUE (MO) AURA BEDARD'S FIRESIDE CHAT INTERVIEW

https://www.firesidechats.ca/video/monique-aura-bedard

Monique (Mo) Aura Bedard is from Oneida Nation of Thames and grew up just outside of Aamjiwnaang First Nation. They call themselves an "art maker" instead of an artist as they do a lot of art-related things. Bedard has worked at an art gallery, teaching art classes as an assistant teacher. They also went to college for a fine arts diploma and then transferred to the University of Lethbridge for a year. They eventually moved back to southern Ontario where they took a year off and applied to art therapy school, which they attended in Toronto at the Toronto Art Therapy Institute. They now work in community doing individual art therapy with youth and started a program called "Our Stories, Our Truths."

Play Monique (Mo) Aura Bedard's Fireside Chat Interview or have students read Mo's article in the textbook or on the web site.

To debrief the video, ask the class the following questions:

1. What led Monique to decide to pursue a career in art therapy?
2. Why does Monique say art therapy – or "art as healing" – is effective?
3. What obstacles has Monique faced and how has she overcome them?
4. What message would Monique give to her younger self if she could?

In Monique (Mo) Aura's interview, they talk about their passion for art therapy. Inform students that they will be guided through a series of art therapy activities in the next section!

APPLY: ART THERAPY ACTIVITIES

Inform students that they will have the opportunity to explore some art therapy activities. These are examples of healthy coping strategies! Students need to choose a minimum of one activity to try but can certainly complete more if they would like to.

Hand out the "Art Therapy Activities Menu" sheet to students, which explains the activities and their intended purpose. Review together as a class.

Allow students time to work on their art activities.

ASSESS:

The Think/Pair/Share activity a form of formative assessment. Teachers will be able to check students' prior knowledge about coping strategies and correct any misconceptions students may have about the topic as students share their answers with their partners and the class.

The debriefing questions after Monique's interview is a form of formative assessment. Teachers will be able to check what students took away from Monique's video and make connections to the other parts of the lesson.

The Art Therapy Activity is a form of summative assessment. How students are assessed (if at all) is up to the teacher's discretion. Teachers are encouraged to meet with students one-on-one to have students explain the meaning of their pieces. If teachers notice any concerning behaviour - such as students art pieces displaying signs of depression or another mental health concern – teachers should talk with students about their feelings, refer students to the school counsellor and periodically check in with students, offering additional mental health resources as necessary.

Choose at least one activity described below.

Vision Board

A Vision Board is a collage of images, words and phrases that represent your vision for your future. Your vision board can include the qualities you want to possess (such as courage or brilliance); your goals for the future; how you want to give back to society; things on your life bucket list; what you want your future to look, feel and sound like etc.

Purpose: Visualizing your future is a powerful tool that influences our feelings, thoughts and ultimately our actions. If you have a clear vision for your future, you are more likely to choose actions and behaviours that will lead you to create that future!

Steps: Cut out images and words (or letters to create your own words) from magazines and paste them onto a piece of poster paper. Once you're done, allow it to dry. Hang your vision board in your room or somewhere you will see it every day.

Emotion Wheel

An Emotion Wheel is a circle divided it into 8 sections, each visually representing a different type of emotion such happy, bored, jealous, scared, loved, curious etc.

Purpose: The Emotion Wheel activity provides an artistic outlet for exploring and processing our emotions. Sitting with an emotion and then visualizing it as an art form is a powerful way to identify and reflect on how our emotions affect us.

Steps: Draw a large circle on a piece of paper or poster board. Divide the circle into eight pie pieces. Choose your eight "big" emotions. Which emotions do you feel the most? Make sure to include a balance of positive and negative emotions. Label each pie piece with a different emotion, writing the emotion on the outside of the pie. Next, start with one emotion. Sit with that emotion, like you are feeling it in the moment. Sometimes it helps to think of a particular time when you felt that emotion so that all those feelings come back. Then, draw a representation of that emotion using colours, lines, and symbols. If that emotion was a piece of art, what would it look like? Repeat this process until your emotion wheel is complete.

Self Portraits

The Self Portraits activity involves drawing three abstract portraits of yourself – how you currently see yourself, how you think others see you, and how you would like to be seen.

Purpose: By creating a series of abstract self-portraits, we are getting to know ourselves on a deeper level. We are forced to ask ourselves tough questions relating to how we perceive ourselves, how others perceive us and how we want to be. This activity has the potential to transform the way we see ourselves.

Steps: Divide your poster board or paper into three sections. In the first section you will draw a representation of how you currently see yourself. Do not get caught up in your physical attributes – this activity is made to represent how you feel about yourself. You may want to simply draw an outline of yourself in each section and fill the inside with colours, lines, images, words etc. In the second section you will draw a representation of how you think others currently see you. What qualities do you think others notice in you? Finally, in the third section, you will draw a representation of how you would like to be seen. Think of this section as your ideal future self. What qualities would you possess? What feelings would you have? How will you affect others? Etc.

Gratitude Tree

A Gratitude Tree drawing is a drawing of a tree, where each leaf includes the name of something or someone you are grateful for.

Purpose: Taking the time to reflect on all the things we are grateful for in life can literally change the neuropathways in our brains to help us develop a more positive mindset. Reflecting on all the things we are grateful for can uplift our mood and help break the pattern of automatic negative thinking.

Steps: On a poster board or piece of paper, draw a tree. Make sure to draw it so that it has many branches and leaves. On each leaf, write one thing you are grateful for. It can be a person, place, experience, gift, item, personal quality, resource etc. Although it may be hard to think of a big list, one you get going you might be surprised about how many things you there are to be grateful for! Make sure to hang this in your room or somewhere you can read it when you are feeling down.

Optional Activity:
If none of the above activities interest you, you can create your own art piece.

Steps: Create your own piece of art and explain to the teacher why you chose to do this, what the purpose was and how it helped you.

Lesson Two: Hanwakan Blakie Whitecloud

Activity: Careers in Filmmaking

CURRICULUM CONNECTIONS	**Alberta, Northwest Territories and Nunavut:** • Entrepreneurship 11 • Entrepreneurship 12 • Knowledge and Employability **British Columbia and Yukon:** • https://curriculum.gov.bc.ca/curriculum/adst/10/entrepreneurship-and-marketing • Career-Life Education **Ontario:** • Career Studies • Business Studies 9,10 • Business Studies 11,12
DURATION	1-2 hours
OVERVIEW	Throughout this lesson, students will explore jobs and careers in the film industry. Students will begin by completing a Quick Write in which they will describe their dream job. Next, students will watch Hanwakan Blakie Whitecloud's Fireside Chat interview where he discusses his journey becoming a filmmaker. Finally, students will brainstorm all the jobs and careers involved in the film industry and be assigned one to research the job description, level of education needed and salary range. The teacher will compile all the answers, so students have a master list describing the careers involved in the film industry!
MATERIALS	• Computer/Projector • Access to individual computer devices and the internet • "Film Industry Mini-Research Assignment" worksheet

Lesson Plan

ACTIVATE: QUICK WRITE

Inform the class that we are going to start the lesson with a Quick Write. A Quick Write is an activity where students quickly write whatever comes to mind about a topic you give them. Typically, students are allotted 3-5 minutes for this activity.

Pose the question "What would your dream job be like?". Allow students 3-5 minutes to write either in point form or paragraph form whatever comes to mind. Some students will likely have specific jobs in mind that they will be describing, while others may be creating a dream job description.

Once the time limit is up, solicit volunteers to share their answers with the class. Ask students to raise their hands if any of their Quick Writes included something about "fun".

Inform the class that today we are going to be learning about Hanwakan Blakie Whitecloud's journey finding a career that he considers fun!

ACQUIRE: HANWAKAN BLAKIE WHITECLOUD'S FIRESIDE CHAT INTERVIEW

https://www.firesidechats.ca/video/hanwakan-blaikie-whitecloud

Hanwakan Blakie Whitecloud is Dakota from Sioux Valley in western Manitoba. An emerging film director, business graduate, outdoor enthusiast and skateboarder; Hanwakan pursues projects with passion and dedication in both his professional and personal life. Film projects include webisodes 'How the art of skateboarding can also be an act of empowerment' & 'Colonialism Skateboards', two web series 'True To The Land' & 'Living By The Drum' and two hour-long documentaries 'The Road To Here', and 'Star People' which will be aired by Aboriginal Peoples Television Network in the fall of 2020. Hanwakan regularly teaches videography, photography and storytelling workshops for youth and regularly curates Indigenous content for educational programming.

Play Hanwakan Blakie Whitecloud's Fireside Chat Interview. As an alternative, students can also read his story in the textbook or on the web site.

To debrief the video, ask the class the following questions:

1. What jobs has Hanwakan had in the past?
2. What does Hanwakan say motivated him to get into filmmaking?
3. What was Hanwakan's educational journey like? What some of his ideas about how education can be improved?
4. How did Hanwakan overcome obstacles in his life?
5. What advice would Hanwakan give his younger self?

In Hanwakan's interview, he talks about his filmmaking career. Inform students that they will have the opportunity to research all the careers involved in the film industry.

APPLY: CAREERS IN FILMMAKING MINI-RESEARCH ASSIGNMENT

Inform students that they will have the opportunity to brainstorm and research all the careers involved in the film industry.

Begin this part of the lesson by having the class brainstorm a list of all the careers and jobs involved in the film industry. Write all the answers on the board. If students are struggling to think of answers, have them watch the credits at the end of a short film or music video. *Possible answers include actors/actresses, directors, writer, camera crew, lighting crew etc.*

Next, assign each student a job or career from the list they brainstormed to research. Distribute the "Film Industry Mini-Reasearch Assignment" worksheet. Each student will be responsible for researching one career/job in the film industry and providing an overview of the job description, level of education needed and salary range. Teachers can assign students the careers they will be responsible for researching or students can choose them themselves (no duplicates though). Students should use the internet as their main source of information, with an emphasis on Canadian and provincial job information.

Examples of relevant career exploration websites:

- Service Canada Job Bank at https://www.jobbank.gc.ca/home
- Career Cruising at www.careercruising.com (subscription needed)
- Alberta Alis at https://alis.alberta.ca/occinfo/wages-and-salaries-in-alberta/
- Ontario Work Info Net at http://onwin.ca/en/careerplanning/

Once students have completed their mini-research assignment, compile all their answers on a shared handout or shared online document for all to see and reference.

Allow students time to review the shared handout or online document.

Finally, ask students to turn to a partner and reflect on the specific filmmaking job or career they would most like to have (if they had to pick one) and why. Alternatively, students can complete a written reflection to be handed in for assessment.

ASSESS:

The Quick Write activity is a form of formative assessment. Teachers will be able to identify where students are at in terms of their career aspirations.

The debriefing questions after Hanwakan's interview is a form of formative assessment. Teachers will be able to check what students took away from his video and make connections to the other parts of the lesson.

The mini-research assignment is a form of summative assessment. Teachers will be able to assess whether students were able to correctly describe the careers including job description, level of education needed and salary range and use relevant sources based on their locations. Teachers may assess for level of completion, accuracy of information and relevance of information.

FILM INDUSTRY MINI-RESEARCH ASSIGNMENT

Use this space to record your research about the job or career you have been assigned. You can use point form notes or paragraph form to record your findings. Make sure to use relevant sources related to your location. Don't forget to cite your sources!

Job/Career: _____

Job Overview	A Day in the Life
Source:	Source:
Level of Education Needed	**Salary Range**
Source:	Source:

Lesson Three: Nooks Lindell

Activity: Indigenous Creatives Mini-Research Assignment

CURRICULUM CONNECTIONS	Alberta, Northwest Territories and Nunavut: • Entrepreneurship 11 • Entrepreneurship 12 • Knowledge and Employability British Columbia and Yukon: • Entrepreneurship and Marketing 10 • Career-Life Education Ontario: • Career Studies • Business Studies 9,10 • Business Studies 11,12
DURATION	1-2 hours
OVERVIEW	Throughout this lesson, students will learn about the Inuit design company - Hinaani Designs - and learn from the creative lead and designer, Nooks Lindell. Students will have the opportunity to explore their website and then watch Nooks' Fireside Chat interview where he discusses the challenges of leaving his home community and how he uses art to balance his mental health. Finally, students will choose an Indigenous creative to research and create an artist profile poster on which will be displayed around the classroom as a source of inspiration and positive Indigenous representation.
MATERIALS	• Computer/Projector • Access to individual computer devices and the internet • "Indigenous Creative Profile" worksheet

Lesson Plan

ACTIVATE: HINAANI DESIGNS WEBSITE EXPLORATION

To begin the lesson, guide students through the Hinaani Designs website at https://www.hinaani.ca, or alternatively, allow students time to individually view the website on their personal devices.

Ask students the following information:

1. Who are the people behind Hinaani Designs?
2. What does "Hinaani" mean?
3. What kind of art do they create?
4. What do you learn about their values?
5. What is your overall impression of their company?

Inform students that next, they will hear from the creative lead and designer, Nooks Lindell.

ACQUIRE: NOOKS LINDELL'S FIRESIDE CHAT INTERVIEW

https://www.firesidechats.ca/video/nooks-lindell

Nooks Lindell is the creative lead and designer at Hinaani Design, a collaboration of creative minded individuals from the Kivalliq region of Nunavut. The team engages in various modern design projects that reflect the culture, language, and land of Inuit. Hinaani sells clothing and accessories featuring their unique print designs as well as handcrafted jewelry and knives that feature locally sourced materials such as ivory, bone and antler. Nooks is an Inuk artist and grew up in Arviat on the shores of Hudson's Bay. He continues to live there with his family. He is actively regaining fluency of his first language, Inuktitut, through family, friends and art. Nooks also participates in traditional Inuit activities; he creates traditional tools, hunts/fishes and is learning to sew with sealskin.

Play Nooks Lindell's Fireside Chat Interview, or provide students time to read his story in the textbook or on the web site.

To debrief the video, ask the class the following questions:

1. What does Nooks say motivated him to start Hinaani Designs?
2. How did Nooks and the Hinaani team get started?
3. What does Nooks say about leaving his home community?
4. What obstacles did Nook face and how did he overcome it?
5. What does Nooks say about Indigenous stories?
6. How does Nooks keep his mental health in check?

In Nooks' interview, he talks about how his passion for art is a strategy to help him overcome his obstacles in life. Inform students that next, they will be researching other Indigenous creatives.

APPLY: INDIGENOUS CREATIVES MINI-RESEARCH ASSIGNMENT

Inform students that they will have the opportunity to brainstorm and research another Indigenous creative. An "Indigenous creative" is another name for an artist, designer or someone who makes cultural items such as jewellery or clothing.

Students can pick an Indigenous creative whom they are familiar with, or one from the "arts/graphic arts" section of the Create to Learn website.

Students can use internet sources such as videos, social media pages, websites for their research- or - if the person is a local Indigenous creative, they may want to interview them.

Hand out the "Indigenous Creative Profile" worksheet. Students will need to research the following information:

1. The person's background/history
2. A description of the art the person creates
3. The person's source(s) of inspiration
4. An overview of the person's social media presence
5. An interesting fact
6. A picture of the person and/or their art

Next, students can use an online program such as Canva to create a poster including all the same information (although the writing can be on a separate page). If possible, print student posters in colour.

Once complete, display the worksheets or posters around the class for everyone to see. The purpose of displaying the profiles around the classroom is so Indigenous art and design role models are represented and a source of inspiration for students.

ASSESS:

The website exploration questions are a form of formative assessment. Teachers can check students understanding of the Hinaani brand.

The debriefing questions after Nooks' interview is a form of formative assessment. Teachers will be able to check what students took away from his video and make connections to the other parts of the lesson.

The mini-research assignment is a form of summative assessment. Teachers will be able to assess whether students were able to complete research about an Indigenous creative, synthesizing their background/history, a description of their art, source of inspiration, and overview of social media presence. Teachers may assess for level of completion, accuracy of information and relevance of information. The worksheet is out of 18 marks.

INDIGENOUS CREATIVE MINI-RESEARCH ASSIGNMENT

Use this space to record your research about an Indigenous creative. You can use point form notes or paragraph form to record your findings. Make sure to use relevant sources related to your location. Don't forget to cite your sources! (18 marks)

Indigenous Creative: _____

Picture:

(3 marks)

Source:

Background/History (3 marks)	About their Art (3 marks)
Source:	Source:

Source of Inspiration	Overview of Social Media Presence
(3 marks)	(3 marks)
Source:	Source:

An Interesting Fact (3 marks):

Source:

Lesson One: Carson Roche

Activity: Indigenous Games

CURRICULUM CONNECTIONS	**Alberta, Northwest Territories and Nunavut:** • Aboriginal Studies Grades 10-12 • Environmental and Outdoor Education Grade 9 • Physical Education 10, 20, 30 **British Columbia and Yukon:** • Contemporary Indigenous Studies Grade 12 • Physical and Health Education 9 • Physical and Health Education 10 • Active Living 11 • Outdoor Education 12 • Active Living 12 **Ontario:** • First Nations, Metis, and Inuit Studies Grades 9-12 • Health and Physical Education 9-12
DURATION	1-2 hours
OVERVIEW	Throughout this lesson, students will learn about traditional Indigenous games, including the North American Indian Games and the Arctic Winter Games. Students will hear from Indigenous sports role model Carson Roche, who utilized sports to deal with the challenges of growing up in a small community and now travels across Canada to isolated communities to teach about traditional Indigenous games! Finally, students will have the opportunity to play some Indigenous games and discuss the purpose of each.
MATERIALS	• Computer/Projector/Internet Connection • Materials to play Indigenous games: Sticks (one for each student), ball, string, tape, rocks or bean bags

Lesson Plan

☀ ACTIVATE: VIDEO CLIPS

To begin this lesson, ask students which sports events they watch. Answers might include NBA games, NHL games, NFL games, community sports events, the Olympics etc.

Ask students to raise their hands if they've ever watched the North American Indigenous Games. What about the Arctic Winter Games?

Inform the group that today the focus of the lesson will be on Indigenous games.

Show students this short video clip describing the history of the North American Indigenous Games: https://www.youtube.com/watch?v=9IB5-EBTzVc

Next, show students this short video clip describing the 2020 Arctic Winter Games: https://www.youtube.com/watch?v=8Eg2-TrLf54

Alternatively, teachers can choose other videos to watch showcasing the North American Indigenous Games and the Arctic Winter Games.

Teachers are encouraged to debrief the videos, asking students what they think and which events they would be interested in participating in.

Inform students that today they will be hearing from Carson Roche, an Indigenous role model in the world of sports!

ACQUIRE: CARSON ROCHE FIRESIDE CHAT INTERVIEW

https://www.firesidechats.ca/video/carson-roche

Carson Roche is from Déline, Northwest Territories. He is a member of the Déline First Nations community. He currently resides in Yellowknife and is the Program Coordinator for the Aboriginal Sports Circle of the NWT. Carson's job allows him to access remote Indigenous communities largely in NWT and the rest of Canada to help encourage youth to participate in sport and traditional games.

Play Carson Roche's Fireside Chat Interview, or give students time to read his story in the textbook or on the web site.

To debrief the video, ask the class the following questions:

1. Why did Carson leave his home community in grade 8?
2. How does Carson say he dealt with the challenges of growing up in a small town?
3. What sport did Carson play in university (for the university sports team)?
4. How did Carson get involved with the Aboriginal Sports Circle?
5. What is Carson's favourite place he's been to and why?
6. What advice does Carson give to youth leaving their home communities?
7. Who is Carson's role model?

In Carson's interview, he talks about teaching Indigenous games. Tell students that next, they will be playing some traditional Indigenous games!

APPLY: INDIGENOUS GAMES

Inform students that they will have the opportunity to play some traditional Indigenous games. Traditional Indigenous games were typically games "introduced to children by Elders to help them learn and develop skills necessary for survival, building strength and agility, hunting and gathering food in harsh weather environments. Many of these active games will also help children increase their physical activity levels while strengthening their sense of culture and tradition"[1].

Below are some examples of traditional Indigenous games which can be played either indoors or outdoors (although you'll need a larger space if playing indoors such as a gym or community centre).

After each game, ask students what purpose the games might have played for the Indigenous nations who invented them. Answers might include developing endurance for travelling, enhancing coordination for hunting etc.

Screaming Eagle
Indigenous Nation: Ojibwe and Arapaho
Equipment Needed: 1 Stick for each player
Skills Tested: Lung Capacity

Steps:

1. Divide the class into two teams. Each team forms a line.
2. The person at the front of the line will go first. When a signal by the teacher is given – such as yelling "go" or "screaming eagle" – the first player of each line holds their stick up in the air, takes a deep breathe in and starts running while screaming "ahhhh".

---

[1] High Five. "Indigenous Games for Children: From Indigenous Communities Across Canada". Founded by Parks and Recreation Ontario. https://www.nscrd.com/uploads/document/files/indigenous-games-for-children-en.pdf

3. Once they run out of breath and stop screaming, players must stop where they are, placing their stick where they ran out of breath.
4. The next players in line will then do the same thing when the teacher gives the signal.
5. The process is repeated until everyone has had a turn.
6. The team who has the farthest stick wins!

Adapted from Robillard, Blair. Playing with a Great Heart: Restoring the Original Intent of Play Though Indigenous Games and Activities. Manitoba Aboriginal Sports and Recreation Council. 2019.

One-Foot-High Kick Game
Indigenous Nation: Inuit
Equipment Needed: String, Ball, Tape
Skills Tested: Explosive Strength, Coordination, Body Control

Steps:

1. Set up targets suspended using string at various heights. It is suggested that there are targets 1 meter off the ground, 1.5 meters and 2 meters. Traditional targets were made from seal skin stuffed with soft material, but a ball or balloon will work fine.
2. Lead students through a leg stretch before attempting this game.
3. Once warmed up, students can take turns practicing touching the targets with their feet.
4. To make the game more exciting, students can run toward the target, take off from both feet and attempt to touch or kick the target with one foot only.
5. The challenge is that students need to land on the same foot they kicked with!

See a video demonstration here: https://www.youtube.com/watch?v=bAehvp7SdcA

Adapted from "Origin of the Arctic Winter Games". Canadian History and Society Through the Lens of Sport. http://canadasports150.ca/en/arctic-winter-games/origin-of-the-arctic-winter-games/77

Make the Stick Jump
Indigenous Nation: Blackfoot
Equipment Needed: Sticks, Rocks or Bean Bags, String
Skills Tested: Accuracy

Steps:

1. Use string to make a line across an open area. This is the line students will have to stand behind.
2. Place sticks on the other side of the line, some close to the line and some far. Assign each stick a point value. Sticks closest to the students can be 1 point and sticks farthest can be 10 points etc.
3. Place rocks or bean bags in a pile. Students will take turns picking up a rock or bean bag, throwing it at a stick of their choosing, trying to make the stick "jump" by hitting the end of it. If the stick jumps, the student gets the point.
4. Have students take turns throwing the rocks or bean bags, remembering their points.
5. At the end of the game, whoever has the most points wins!

Adapted from: High Five. "Indigenous Games for Children: From Indigenous Communities Across Canada". Founded by Parks and Recreation Ontario. https://www.nscrd.com/uploads/document/files/indigenous-games-for-children-en.pdf

ASSESS:

The debriefing questions after the activating video clips, Carson's interview, and the games are formative assessments. Teachers will be able to determine what students learned and how they felt playing the games!

Lesson Two: Richard Pellissier-Lush

Activity: Positive Sportsmanship

CURRICULUM CONNECTIONS	Alberta, Northwest Territories and Nunavut:
	<ul><li>Aboriginal Studies Grades 10-12:</li><li>Environmental and Outdoor Education Grade 9:</li><li>Physical Education 10, 20, 30</li></ul>
	British Columbia and Yukon:
	<ul><li>Contemporary Indigenous Studies Grade 12</li><li>Physical and Health Education 9 and 10</li><li>Active Living 11 and 12</li><li>Outdoor Education 12</li></ul>
	Ontario:
	<ul><li>First Nations, Metis, and Inuit Studies Grades 9-12:</li><li>Health and Physical Education 9-12</li></ul>
DURATION	1-2 hours
OVERVIEW	Throughout this lesson, students will be making connections between the Seven Sacred Teachings and positive sportsmanship. First, students will learn about the Seven Sacred teachings and watch examples of positive sportsmanship from the Olympics. Students will identify which teaching was utilized in each example from the Olympics. Next, students will learn from Indigenous sports role model, Richard Pellissier-Lush. Finally, students will be assigned one of the Seven Sacred Teachings and will work in groups to role-play a sports scenario in which they utilize that teaching by demonstrating positive sportsmanship.
MATERIALS	<ul><li>Computer/Projector/Internet Connection</li><li>Pages 10-14 of the Free Online Resource "Seven Grandfather Teachings: Character Development" found at https://rover.edonline.sk.ca/system/guides/R054842.pdf</li></ul>

Lesson Plan

☀ ACTIVATE: SEVEN SACRED TEACHINGS AND SPORTING EXAMPLES

Inform students that today's lesson is all about sports and positive sportsmanship. To begin, ask students what "positive sportsmanship" could look like. Possible answers may include giving teammates encouragement or shaking hands with the opposing team at the end of the game.

Next, ask students if they can name the Seven Sacred Teachings, according to Anishinaabe (or other Indigenous nation) worldview. If possible, it is encouraged to invite a local Elder or Knowledge teacher into the class to give a nation-specific teaching, if applicable in your region.

Alternatively, you can review pages 10-14 of the "Seven Grandfather Teachings: Character Development" together as a class, found at: https://rover.edonline.sk.ca/system/guides/R054842.pdf

Next, show students the YouTube video "Top 10 Moments of Olympic Sporting Spirit" here: https://www.youtube.com/watch?v=3SuKNmLBOpE . After each example in the video, stop and ask students which of the seven sacred teachings was demonstrated.

Debrief the video by asking students which instance of positive sportsmanship stood out to them and why.

Inform them that next, they are going to learn from Indigenous sports role model, Richard Pellissier-Lush.

ACQUIRE: RICHARD PELLISSIER-LUSH'S FIRESIDE CHAT INTERVIEW

https://www.firesidechats.ca/video/richard-pellissier-lush

Richard Lush is a Mi'kmaq man from Lennox Island First Nation, PEI. His passions are based on his Mi'kmaq culture, traditions, loyalty and love of the First Nations communities and his family, the Mi'kmaq people. He previously worked with the PEI Aboriginal Sport Circle and was heavily involved with the two First Nation Communities here in PEI, his biggest strength is working with his Mi'kmaq brothers and sisters. Richard graduated and was selected to be the Valedictorian of his 2012 Sport & Leisure Management Program, and continued his Education at the University of Manitoba. Richard has converted his skills he learned through education, as skills to creating opportunities for the First Nation Communities in PEI to thrive, preserve, and educate Indigenous and non Indigenous people across Mikjikj Mniku (Turtle Island). Richard is one of the founders and original members of Mi'kmaq Legends (Mi'kmaq Heritage Actors), an all Indigenous Theatre Group that specializes in telling the stories, traditions, songs, dances, and culture of the Mi'kmaq from the past, and present.

Play Richard Pellissier-Lush's Fireside Chat Interview, or provide students time to read his story in the textbook or on the web site.

To debrief the video, ask the class the following questions:

1. What are some of Richard's passions and interests?
2. How did Richard make sure he stayed on a good path?
3. How did Richard secure a chance to try-out for the University of Manitoba's football team?
4. What was Richard's education journey like?
5. What advice does Richard have for youth?
6. How has Richard demonstrated each of the seven sacred teachings throughout his life?

In Richard's interview, he talks about his passion for theatre and helping his community. Inform students that in the next part of the lesson, they will be utilizing theatre to learn about sportsmanship.

APPLY: ROLE PLAYING

Inform students that in this activity, they will be role-playing ways the Seven Sacred Teachings can be utilized in various situations in sports and demonstrating how to be a good teammate by engaging in positive sportsmanship. Remind them to think of the examples of good sportsmanship they came up with in the activating activity, as well as the video they watched.

Next, divide students into groups of 3-4. Assign each team one of the Seven Sacred Teachings. Teams will have 10 minutes to brainstorm a scenario where the teaching can be applied and practice acting out their response. For example, if a team is assigned the teaching "humility", they have to think of a scenario where a teammate demonstrates humility such as passing the ball to a teammate in the final seconds of a close basketball game, rather than attempting the shot by themselves.

Once teams are done, have them act out their scenarios for the class while other teams guess what the situation is and which teaching they are demonstrating. After each team showcases their role-playing scenarios, ask the other groups what they thought of the group's response – in what ways did it demonstrate positive sportsmanship? Which of the seven sacred teachings was utilized? How can you apply this teaching in other situations outside of sports?

Once everyone has had a turn thank students for taking a risk and engaging in the activity!

ASSESS:

The debriefing questions after the activating activity and Richard's video are forms of formative assessment. Teachers will be able to check what students took away from the videos and make connections to the other parts of the lesson.

The role-playing activity is also a form of formative assessment. Teachers will be able to see if groups understand what positive sportsmanship looks like by utilizing the Seven Sacred Teachings and correct any misconceptions students have.

Lesson One: Jessica Dumas

Activity: Exploring Beliefs about Money

CURRICULUM CONNECTIONS	**Alberta, Northwest Territories and Nunavut:** • Aboriginal Studies Grades 10-12 • Knowledge and Employability ELA10-4 • Career and Life Management • Fin1010: Personal Financial Management **British Columbia and Yukon:** • Contemporary Indigenous Studies Grade 12 • Foundations of Mathematics 11 • Workplace Mathematics 11 • Precalculus 11 • Accounting 11 • Accounting 12 **Ontario:** • First Nations, Metis, and Inuit Studies Grades 9-12 • Career Studies 10 • Busines Studies 9,10 • Entrepreneurship 11,12
DURATION	1-2 Hours
OVERVIEW	In this lesson, students will explore and transform their personal beliefs about money. Students will first engage in an agree/disagree activity, comparing their personal beliefs with the rest of the class. Next, students will learn from Indigenous life and business coach, Jessica Dumas, about her struggles, career and philosophy about money and finances. Finally, students will independently complete a workbook transforming their ideas about money and setting financial goals for the future.
MATERIALS	• Computer/Projector/Internet Access • Student Devices with internet • "Beliefs About Money Workbook" • Writing Utensils, Pencil Crayons, Markers

Lesson Plan

☀ ACTIVATE: AGREE/DISAGREE ACTIVITY

To begin this lesson, without giving any context, designate one side of the classroom as the "agree" side, and the opposite side as the "disagree" side. Have students gather in the middle of the class, and when you read out a statement, instruct them to move to the "agree" side if they agree with the statement or the "disagree" side if they disagree with the statement. Inform students there are no right or wrong answers, only personal opinions.

After students have picked a side, you may want to ask a student from each side to volunteer why they chose the side they did.

Statements:

1. Money is the source of all evil.
2. I can never have enough money.

3. Money is the solution to all my problems.
4. Money should be managed.
5. Financial literacy is important. *Financial literacy is having the knowledge, skills and confidence to make responsible financial decisions*[1]
6. I love money.
7. Money is a tool for me to build the future I want.
8. Money makes people greedy.
9. Money makes people generous.
10. Saving money is important.
11. Money will make me happy.
12. To make money you must take financial risks.

Inform students that today's lesson is going to be all about – you guessed it – money! Explain that the agree/disagree activity was to gauge their beliefs about money. Inform students that there are no right or wrong answers, but what is important is that we are reflecting on how we think about money.

Inform students that next they will hear from Indigenous life and business coach, Jessica Dumas.

ACQUIRE: JESSICA DUMAS' FIRESIDE CHAT VIDEO

https://www.firesidechats.ca/video/jessica-dumas

Jessica Dumas is a certified life and business coach who is passionate about helping women and entrepreneurs live more confidently and independently in owning self-love. Jessica recognizes how our personal growth stimulates our impact on our community. She is a sought-after speaker in the areas of women in business, leadership success and Indigenous inclusion. Jessica is an award winning professional and avid volunteer. She is currently serving as the first Indigenous Female to Chair the Winnipeg Chamber of Commerce, and she has served as the Chairperson for the Aboriginal Chamber of Commerce, as well as many other board positions over the years. She is a powerful role model and advocate for self-love and social justice, by the shocking and sudden loss of her brother in 2005, into an opportunity to overcome hardship by developing personal strengths, vision and self-confidence and demonstrating her own story of reconciliation.

Play Jessica Dumas' Fireside Chat Video or have students read the textbook chapter.

To debrief the video, ask the class the following questions:

1. What was Jessica's school experience like?
2. What jobs has Jessica had?
3. What trauma has Jessica experienced and how did she deal with it?
4. What does Jessica say about university?
5. What are some of the business challenges Jessica faces now?
6. What does Jessica say about money? How does this confirm or challenge some of your own beliefs about money?
7. What advice does Jessica give at the end?

Students will use Jessica's advice about money to shape their thinking about the topic to develop a healthy relationship with money.

---

1 Government of Canada. "Financial Literacy Background". https://www.canada.ca/en/financial-consumer-agency/programs/financial-literacy/financial-literacy-history.html

APPLY: BELIEFS ABOUT MONEY WORKBOOK

Hand out the "Beliefs About Money Workbook". Inform students that they are going to be working independently to explore the concept of money further and set financial goals for themselves.

Students can complete the workbook pages in whatever order they choose.

Cover Page: On the front of the workbook, students will draw images and write words representing their outlook on money (5 marks).

Learning About Money: On this page, students will go through four modules from the Financial Consumer Agency of Canada and then summarize their learning in the space provided (20 marks).

Link: https://www.canada.ca/en/financial-consumer-agency/services/financial-toolkit.html

What Money Can and Cannot Buy: On the second page of the workbook, students will compare what money can and cannot buy. For example, they might write that money can buy expensive medical care but cannot buy health (10 marks).

My Financial Goals: On the third page of the workbook, students will set 10 financial goals for themselves. Encourage students to think of short term, medium term and long-term goals (5 marks).

ASSESS:

The agree/disagree activity is a form of formative assessment. This activity will enable teachers and students to gauge their own and other's personal beliefs about money.

The debriefing questions after Jessica's interview with Fireside Chats is a form of formative assessment. Teachers will be able to check what students took away from the video and make connections to the other parts of the lesson.

The "Beliefs about Money" workbook is a form of summative assessment. Students can be assessed on level of completeness, accuracy of information from the Learning about Money page and thoughtfulness of answers. The workbook is out of 40 marks.

TAKE STUDENT LEARNING FURTHER

Have students create a future budget for themselves. Instruct students to complete internet research finding a suitable place to rent and a suitable method of transportation, plus a budget for food, clothing, entertainment etc. to determine how much money they will need to make per month and year to achieve the lifestyle they want. Have students submit a detailed budget including monthly income and expenses.

BELIEFS ABOUT MONEY WORKBOOK

NAME:

Use this space to draw images and write words representing your beliefs about money. Make sure to include both positive and negative representations. *5 marks*

LEARNING ABOUT MONEY

Use this space to summarize your learning about money by completing four modules found at https://www.canada.ca/en/financial-consumer-agency/services/financial-toolkit.html

5 marks each = 20 marks

Module 1: Income, Expenses and Budget	Module 2: Banking
Module 3: Saving	Module 4: Credit and Debt Management

WHAT MONEY CAN AND CANNOT BUY

Use this space to brainstorm a list of 10 things money can buy and 10 things money cannot buy. Example: Money can buy gifts but cannot buy friendship. *10 marks*

What Money Can Buy	What Money Can't Buy

MY FINANCIAL GOALS

Use this space to write at least ten financial goals you have in your life. *5 marks*

1. I will

2. I will

3. I will

4. I will

5. I will

6. I will

7. I will

8. I will

9. I will

10. I will

Lesson Two: Dana Marlatt

Activity: Hierarchy of Needs

CURRICULUM CONNECTIONS	**Alberta, Northwest Territories and Nunavut:** • Aboriginal Studies Grades 10-12 • Knowledge and Employability ELA10-4 • Career and Life Management • School Health Program, Grade 9 **British Columbia and Yukon:** • Contemporary Indigenous Studies Grade 12 • Career-Life Connections • E-Commerce 12 **Ontario:** • First Nations, Metis, and Inuit Studies Grades 9-12 • Career Studies 10 • Busines Studies 9,10 • Entrepreneurship 11,12
DURATION	1-2 Hours
OVERVIEW	Throughout this lesson, students will learn about human needs according to Maslow's hierarchy. Students will first engage in a stick-note activity where they will work in groups to brainstorm a list of human needs, working together to categorize them into groups. Next, students will hear from Indigenous role model, Dana Marlatt. Finally, students will learn more about Maslow's Hierarchy of needs and complete a worksheet outlining as many businesses and services that work to fulfil peoples' needs!
MATERIALS	• Sticky Notes • Computer/Projector/Internet Access • "Maslow's Hierarchy of Needs" worksheet

Lesson Plan

☀ ACTIVATE: STICKY NOTE ACTIVITY

Hand out 3 sticky notes to each student. Pose the question "what are some examples of human needs". Allow students time to write their answers on the notes. Students should write one answer per note.

Next, divide students into groups of five. In their groups, students should first share their answers. Once everyone has shared their answers, instruct groups to see if they can categorize the responses. Examples of human needs categories can include physical needs, emotional needs etc.

Once groups have categorized all the responses into categories of their choice, ask each group to share the categories they came up with, and share the responses in each category. As groups are taking turns sharing their responses, write the categories on the board, leaving space for students to come put their sticky notes in the correct categories.

Finally, have students come up to the board and place their sticky notes in the correct category.

The purpose of this activity is for students to have examples of human needs for the latter part of the lesson.

Inform students that next they will hear from Indigenous role model, Dana Marlatt.

ACQUIRE: DANA MARLATT'S FIRESIDE CHAT VIDEO

https://www.firesidechats.ca/video/dana-marlatt

Dana Marlatt is from Fort Union, Ontario. Her mom is of German descent and her dad is Woodland Metis. Dana has lived in downtown Toronto for the last six years. She describes that she lost her spirit but found it in the city. Dana started working at a young age and has many jobs including working in the restaurant industry, then as research assistant, working for a staffing start-up company, working at an animal hospital, and finally, working at RBC as part of the Indigenous Peoples Developmental Program.

Play Dana Marlatt's Fireside Chat Video or have students read the textbook chapter.

To debrief the video, ask the class the following questions:

1. How does Dana describe her childhood?
2. What skills does Dana say she learned in the restaurant industry?
3. What is RBC's Indigenous Peoples Developmental Program?
4. How does Dana describe her mindset?
5. What experience does Dana say shook her confidence?
6. What does Dana say about informal education?
7. What does Dana say about mental health?

In her interview, Dana talks about Maslow's Hierarchy of Needs. Inform students that today they will explore this concept including its relationship with business.

APPLY: MASLOW'S HIERARCHY OF NEEDS

Show students a picture of Maslow's Hierarchy of Needs. Pictures can be found on an internet search engine. Inform students that according to Maslow, humans have five categories of needs beginning with physical needs, safety needs, love/belonging, esteem and self-actualization.

Ask groups to reflect the how well the categories they came up with fit with Maslow's categories. What are the similarities? What are the differences?

Next, have a volunteer re-configure the sticky notes on the board to reflect Maslow's Hierarchy. How well do the classes answers fit into Maslow's philosophy? Likely, the answers fit perfectly.

Next, inform students that some people speculate that Maslow came up with his theory based on the fieldwork he did with the Blackfoot nation. In fact, Gitxsan activist for child welfare and executive director of the First Nations Child and Family Caring Society of Canada, Cindy Blackstock, is quoted saying "First of all, the triangle is not a triangle. It's a tipi. And the tipis in the Blackfoot (tradition) always went up and reached up to the skies"[1] Cindy Blackstock explains that in the Blackfoot version, self-actualization is on the bottom of the tipi, followed by community actualization and finally, cultural perpetuity at the top. Regardless of how you think about it, most people agree that humans have basic needs that more or less can fall into one of the five categories that Maslow published based on his work with the Blackfoot nation.

Next, hand out "Maslow's Hierarchy of Needs" worksheet. Instruct students to think about all the

---

[1] Michel, Karen Lincoln. "Maslow's Hierarchy Connected to Blackfoot Beliefs". 9 April 2014. http://mmiwontario.ca/images/Maslow's%20Hierarchy%20Connected%20to%20Blackfoot%20Beliefs.pdf

business and services that exist to fulfil peoples' needs. Students can work independently for 15 minutes, and then compare answers with a friend. Students should think of a minimum of 25 answers, or 5 answers per category.

Finally, ask them if they can think of any business ideas that fulfil community actualization or cultural perpetuity based on Blackfoot philosophies. Once students have finished brainstorming, tell them that the best business ideas are ones that serve a need or fix a problem!

ASSESS:

The sticky notes activity is a form of formative assessment. This activity will enable teachers to assess group learning, prior knowledge, communication, and categorization skills.

The debriefing questions after Dana's interview with Fireside Chats is a form of formative assessment. Teachers will be able to check what students took away from the video and make connections to the other parts of the lesson.

The "Maslow's Hierarchy of Needs" worksheet is a form of summative assessment. Students can be assessed on level of completeness and thoughtfulness of answers. The worksheet can be graded out of 25 marks.

MASLOW'S HIERARCHY OF NEEDS

Label the five categories and fill out this worksheet with all the business and services that exist to fulfil peoples' needs.
25 marks

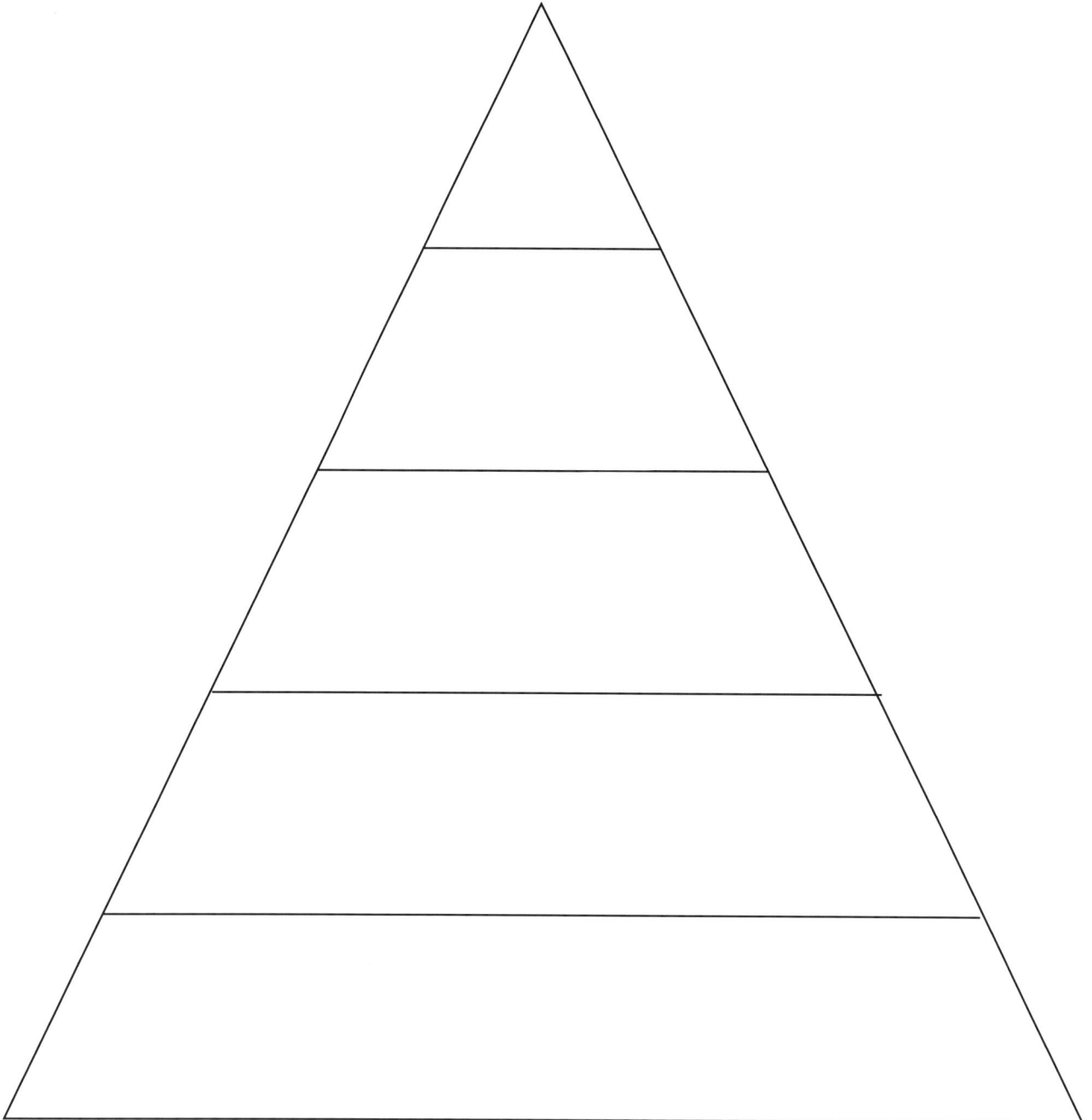

Lesson One: Brianna Oversby

Activity: Found Art

CURRICULUM CONNECTIONS	**Alberta, Northwest Territories and Nunavut:** • Aboriginal Studies Grades 10-12 • Art 10,20,30 • School Health Program, Grade 9 • Career-Life Management **British Columbia and Yukon:** • Contemporary Indigenous Studies Grade 12 • Physical and Health Education 9 • Physical and Health Education Grade 10 **Ontario:** • First Nations, Metis, and Inuit Studies Grades 9-12 • Health and Physical Education 9-12 • Health and Physical Education Grades 9-12 • Personal Life Management Grade 12
DURATION	3-4 Hours
OVERVIEW	In this lesson, students will learn about using art to cope with life's challenges. Students will first engage in a gallery walk where they will view images from Indigenous artist Jobena Petonoquot's exhibit ""Rebellion of my Ancestors" where she uses common objects to create thought-provoking art about residential schools. Next, students will watch Indigenous educator Brianna Oversby's Fireside Chat video where she discusses her love of art and using art to cope with life's challenges. Finally, students will have the opportunity to create their own "found art" piece that represents overcoming challenges. Students will write a reflection describing their art and will be marked using the "Written Reflection" rubric
MATERIALS	• Computer/Projector/Internet • "Gallery Walk Images" • "Found Art" materials (students are responsible for finding items) • Written Reflection Rubric"

Lesson Plan

☀ ACTIVATE: GALLERY WALK

Prior to the beginning of the lesson, print the "Rebellion of my Ancestors Gallery Walk" posters in colour and hang them around the room. Alternatively, have the class view the images online at https://www.dawsoncollege.qc.ca/art-gallery/exhibitions/jobena-petonoquot-rebellion-of-my-ancestors/

Divide students into five groups. Inform them that they will be viewing and learning about "found art" created by Indigenous artist, Jobena Petonoquot. Explain that "found art" is a type of art that uses ordinary items found by the artist to create artistic designs. The examples from today's lesson all come from Indigenous artist Jobena Petonoquot's exhibit called "Rebellion of my Ancestors".

Groups should be given 3-4 minutes to view the posters, discussing the items used, the designs created and their impact on viewers. What do you think each piece is represents? Do you like the art? Why or why not? How does this piece relate to the theme of rebellion? What story does each piece tell about life at residential schools?

Once the time limit is up, groups will rotate to the next poster, until they've had a chance to view each one.

Next, inform the group that they will be learning about using art to cope with life's challenges, by watching Brianna Oversby's Fireside Chat interview.

ACQUIRE: BRIANNA OVERSBY FIRESIDE CHAT VIDEO

https://www.firesidechats.ca/video/brianna-oversby

Brianna Oversby is a Métis/settler queer educator and artist. Oversby grew up riding horses, eating saskatoons and building weird stuff on Treaty 2 Territory under big prairie skies. Currently an Educational Consultant at inPath, Oversby holds a M.Ed. from the Harvard Graduate School of Education and is passionate about building creative learning experiences for youth.

Play Brianna's Fireside Chat Video or have students read the story in the textbook.

To debrief the video, ask the class the following questions:

1. What does Brianna do for work?
2. What jobs has Brianna had in the past?
3. What was Brianna's educational journey like?
4. Where has Brianna lived?
5. What does Brianna say is her biggest motivation?
6. What obstacles has Brianna faced and how does she say she overcame them?
7. What advice does Brianna give youth?

In her interview, Brianna discusses art education as a vehicle to help people process the challenges they face. Inform the class that in the next part of the lesson they will learn about using art to cope with life's challenges.

APPLY: CREATING FOUND ART

Inform the class that today they will be using what they learned about found art in the first section to create their own found art pieces. Their assignment is to create found art that represents overcoming challenges.

Encourage students to find the materials for their art by searching through the recycling bin, their desks, lockers, under their beds, outside etc. for common items that can be transformed into art. Examples of items that can be used include old pencils, paper recycling, leaves, grass, flowers and more!

Allow students 1-2 hours to create their art pieces.

Once finished, have students describe their art pieces in a written reflection. Students should answer the following prompt:

Describe your art piece. What items did you use? How does your art piece represent overcoming challenges? What story does your art piece tell?

Finally, display students' art and reflections around the class and have students engage in a final gallery walk viewing and discussing their peers art.

ASSESS:

The Gallery Walk activity is a form of formative assessment. This activity will enable students to engage in discussions about art, trauma and history.

The debriefing questions after Dr. Glen Sharpe's interview with Fireside Chats is a form of formative assessment. Teachers will be able to check students' comprehension of the topics discussed in the video.

The written reflection is a form of summative assessment. Teachers will be able to assess students' writing and connections to other parts of the lesson.

The final gallery walk is a form of formative assessment. Students will be able to discuss their peers' art and how it relates to the theme of the lesson while celebrating their learning.

Series of 4 beaded baptism gowns, 2018 Photo: Sylvia Trotter Ewens
Found at: https://www.dawsoncollege.qc.ca/art-gallery/exhibitions/jobena-petonoquot-rebellion-of-my-ancestors/

2018 Photo: Sylvia Trotter Ewens
Found at: https://www.dawsoncollege.qc.ca/art-gallery/exhibitions/jobena-petonoquot-rebellion-of-my-ancestors/

2018 Photo: Sylvia Trotter Ewens
Found at: https://www.dawsoncollege.qc.ca/art-gallery/exhibitions/jobena-petonoquot-rebellion-of-my-ancestors/

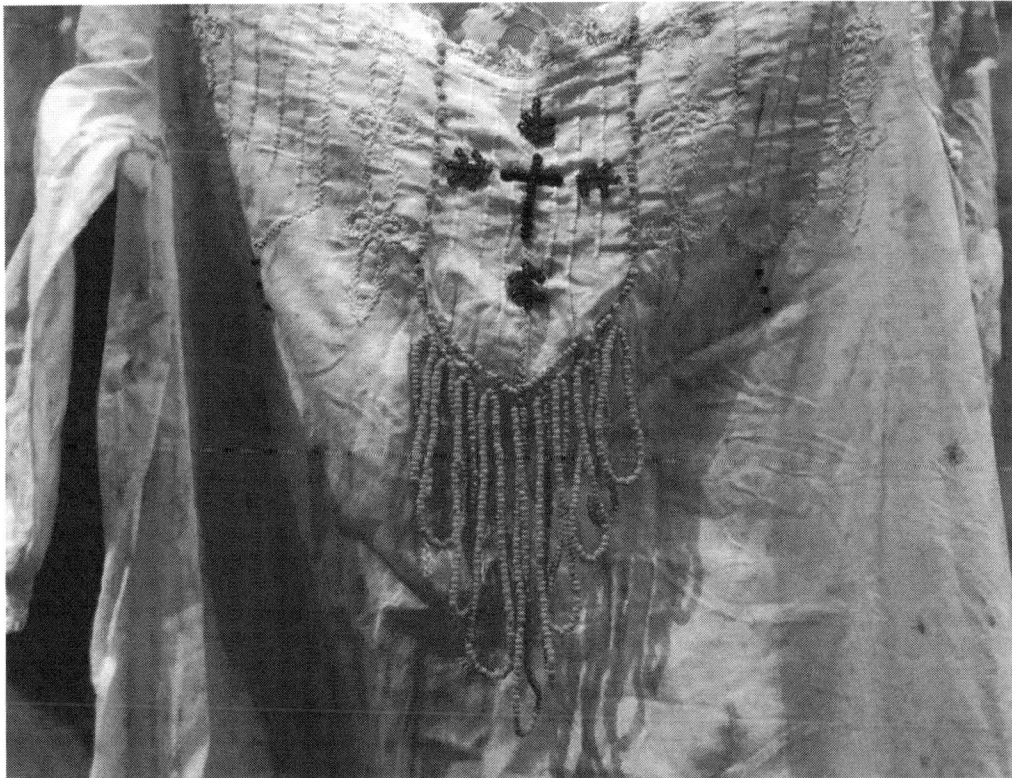

Jessica Deer/CBC found at: https://www.cbc.ca/news/indigenous/jobena-petonoquot-solo-exhibit-montreal-1.4949079

REFLECTION RUBRIC

Reflection Prompts: *Describe your art piece. What items did you use? How does your art piece represent overcoming challenges? What story does your art piece tell?*

	EXCELLENT (5)	GOOD (4)	SATISFACTORY (3-2)	NEEDS IMPROVEMENT (1-0)
Content /5	The author effectively answers the reflection prompts	The author answers the reflection prompts	The author attempts to answer one or more of the reflection prompts	The author does not answer the reflection prompts
Connections /5	The author makes connections between the prompts, other parts of the lesson, personal experience, and prior learning	The author makes connections between the prompts and other parts of the lesson	The author attempts to make connections between the prompts and other parts of the lesson	The author does not attempt to make connections
Depth /5	The author provides an in-depth discussion about found art and overcoming challenges	The author provides an insightful discussion about overcoming challenges	The author provides a simple description of overcoming a challenge	No attempt at in-depth reflection is made

Total = _____ out of 15

Teacher Comments:

Lesson Two: Christine M'Lot

Medicine Wheel Goal Setting

CURRICULUM CONNECTIONS	**Alberta, Northwest Territories and Nunavut:** • Aboriginal Studies Grades 10-12 • School Health Program, Grade 9 • Career-Life Management **British Columbia and Yukon:** • Contemporary Indigenous Studies Grade 12 • Physical and Health Education 9 • Physical and Health Education Grade 10 **Ontario:** • First Nations, Metis, and Inuit Studies Grades 9-12 • Health and Physical Education 9-12 • Health and Physical Education Grades 9-12 • Personal Life Management Grade 12 • Dynamics of Human Relationships Grade 11 • Exploring Family Studies Grades 9-10
DURATION	1-2 Hours
OVERVIEW	Schools often don't explicitly teach students how to be well. Throughout this lesson, students will learn about Indigenous perspectives of wellness relating to all parts of the self: physical, mental, emotional, and spiritual. Students will learn to use a fusion of strategies from Anishinaabe culture and the field of positive psychology to help them set goals in the categories of physical, spiritual, mental, and emotional that they are more likely to accomplish. Students will also learn the value of self-care while developing an understanding and appreciation of Anishinaabe culture and worldview.
MATERIALS	• Sticky Notes • Computer/Projector/Internet • Paper, Pencils • "Medicine Wheel Goal Setting" Template • "Medicine Wheel Goal Setting Checklist"

Lesson Plan

☀ ACTIVATE: STICKY NOTE ACTIVITY

Hand out 3 sticky notes to each student. Pose the question "what are some ways you practice self-care?". Allow students time to write their answers on the notes. Students should write one answer per note.

Next, divide students into groups of five. In their groups, students should first share their answers. Once everyone has shared their answers about how they practice self-care, instruct groups to see if they can categorize the responses. Examples of self-care categories might be "exercise" and "distractions".

Once groups have categorized all the responses into categories, ask each group to share the categories they came up with, and share the responses in each category. As groups are taking turns sharing their responses, write the categories on the board, leaving space for students to come put their sticky notes in the correct categories.

Finally, have students come up to the board and place their sticky notes in the correct category.

The purpose of this activity is for students to have examples of self-care for the latter part of the lesson.

Inform students that next, they will hear from Indigenous educator, Christine M'Lot.

ACQUIRE: CHRISTINE M'LOT'S FIRESIDE CHAT VIDEO

https://www.firesidechats.ca/video/christine-mlot

CHRISTINE M'LOT (she/her/hers) is an award-winning Anishinaabe educator and curriculum developer from Winnipeg, Manitoba. She has experience working with children and youth in multiple capacities including child welfare, children's disAbility services and Indigenous family programming. She currently is teaching high school at the University of Winnipeg Collegiate. Christine is also the co-founder of Red Rising Education, and works to create Indigenous education resources for teacher

Play Christine M'Lot's Fireside Chat Video or have students read the textbook chapter.

To debrief the video, ask the class the following questions:

1. How does Christine describe her education journey?
2. What obstacles does Christine say she faced?
3. Who was Christine's role model and how did he help her stay on a good path?
4. What advice does Christine give to youth?
5. What advice would Christine give her younger self?
6. How does Christine say she keeps her mental health in check?
7. Where does Christine say she draws her inspiration from?

In her interview, Christine talks about her Medicine Wheel Goal Setting activity, which students will be led through in the next part of the lesson!

APPLY: MEDICINE WHEEL GOAL SETTING

Show students Christine's Youtube mini-series "Medicine Wheel Goal Setting". This is a three-part mini-series that will take students through the history of the Medicine Wheel, how to use the Medicine Wheel to set goals and goal setting tips from the field of positive psychology.

Hand out the "Medicine Wheel Goal Setting" template so students can do the activity as they watch the videos.

Part 1: A Brief History of the Medicine Wheel (5 minutes)
Watch here: https://www.youtube.com/watch?v=Z1lOLDTJGJk

In this first video of a three-part series, Christine discusses the history of the Anishinaabe Medicine Wheel, including how long it's been used for, it's meanings and what we can learn from it.

Part 2: Medicine Wheel Goal Setting
Watch here: https://www.youtube.com/watch?v=0N9bI9FSbcA

In this second video, Christine takes you through a goal setting activity, using the Medicine Wheel. Christine discusses mental health, including the difference between healthy and unhealthy coping strategies. You're encouraged to follow along and create your own goals.

Tip: As students are thinking of goals in the "Emotions" category, refer them to the examples they gave in the activating activity.

Part 3: Goal Setting Tips
Watch here: https://www.youtube.com/watch?v=_KDz_nDiNP0

In this third and final video, Christine shares some tips from the field of positive psychology to help you format your goals in a way that increases your chance of achieving them!

ASSESS:

The sticky notes activity is a form of formative assessment. This activity will enable teachers to assess group learning, student communication and categorizing skills.

The debriefing questions after Christine's interview with Fireside Chats is a form of formative assessment. Teachers will be able to check what students took away from the video and make connections to the other parts of the lesson.

The Medicine Wheel Goal Setting activity is a form of summative assessment. Teachers can grade the assignment using the "Medicine Wheel Goal Setting Checklist".

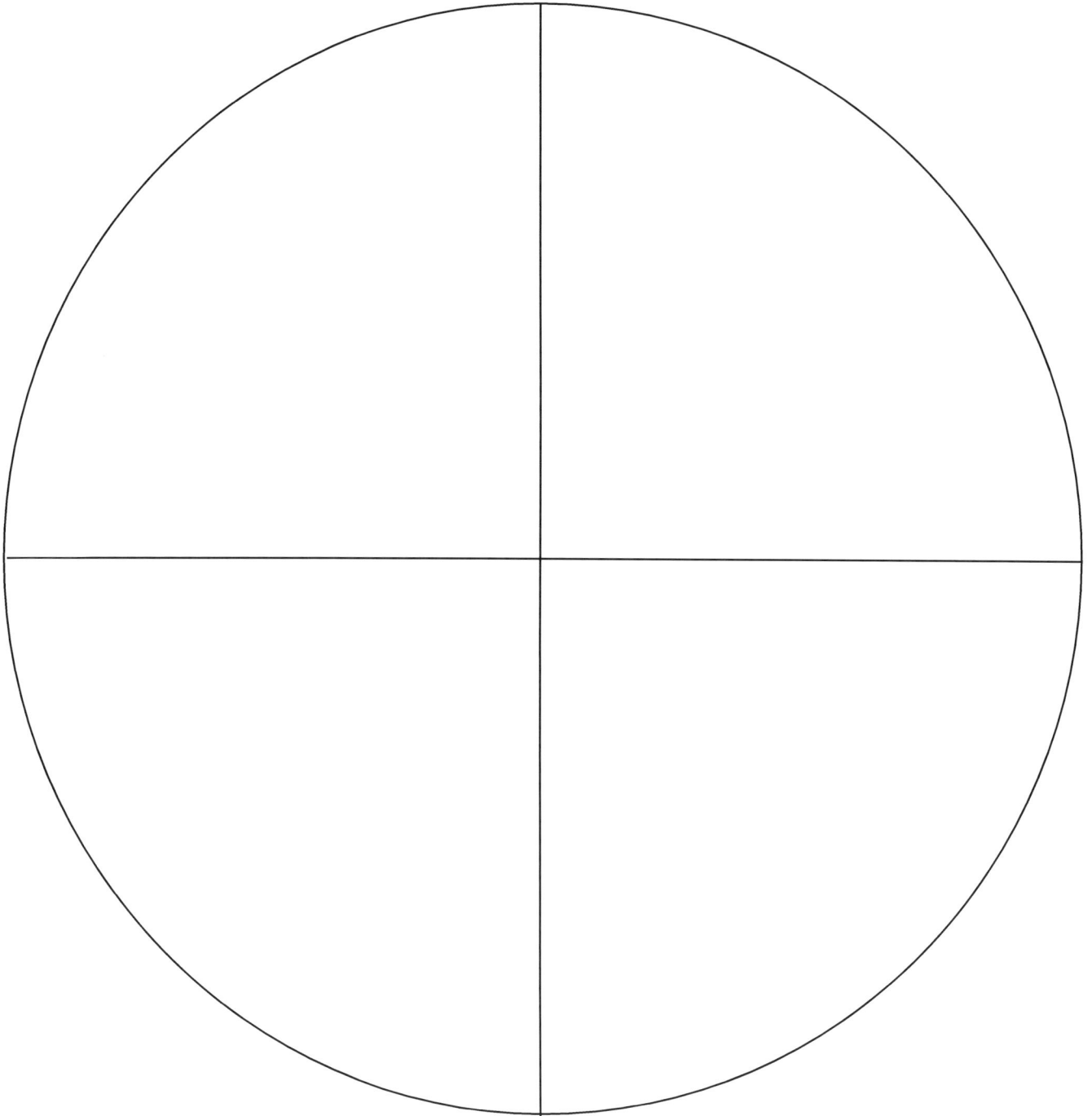

MEDICINE WHEEL GOAL SETTING CHECKLIST

Student has demonstrated they understand the four parts of the self, according to Anishinaabe worldview by setting appropriate goals in each category. /10 marks

Student has set three goals in each category. /5 marks

Goals are set in the SMART goal format. /5 marks

Total = /20 marks

Comments:

Lesson Three: Niigaan Sinclair
Activity: Indigenous Topics

CURRICULUM CONNECTIONS	**Alberta, Northwest Territories and Nunavut:** • Aboriginal Studies Grades 10-12 • English Language Arts Grades 10-12 • English Language Arts Grades 10, 11, 12: Uqausiliriniq Strand **British Columbia and Yukon:** • Contemporary Indigenous Studies Grade 12 • English Language Arts Composition Grades 10, 11, 12 **Ontario:** • First Nations, Metis, and Inuit Studies Grades 9-12 • English Language Arts Grades 9-10 • English Language Arts Grades 11-12
DURATION	1-2 Hours
OVERVIEW	Throughout this lesson, students will learn about Indigenous history and topics in Canada. First, students will work in teams and engage in a fun quiz game to test their prior knowledge about Indigenous history in Canada. Next, students will listen to Niigaan Sinclair's Fireside Chat interview where he talks about his many roles teaching about Indigenous topics in Canada. Finally, students will read one of his editorials published in the *Winnipeg Free Press* titled "Students or Slaves? Work at Residential Schools Under Fire". Students will complete an editorial analysis and write a one-page reflection connecting the article to other parts of the lesson, personal experience, and prior learning.
MATERIALS	• Computer/Projector/Internet • Paper, Pencils • "Students or Slaves?" Article • "Article Analysis" worksheet • "Reflection Rubric"

Lesson Plan

☀ ACTIVATE: INDIGENOUS TOPICS QUIZ

Begin the lesson by engaging the class in a game about Indigenous history and topics in Canada. Divide the class into two teams and have the teams compete to get the most quiz questions correct. Alternatively, use the questions to create an interactive online game on the Kahoot website (http://kahoot.com)

Quiz Questions and Answers:

1. True or False? The name Canada comes from the Huron-Iroquois word "kanata," meaning "village" or "settlement."
Answer: True [1]

2. True or False? Indigenous nations in Canada invented the canoe and kayak.

---

[1] Government of Canada. "Origins of the Name Canada". https://www.canada.ca/en/canadian-heritage/services/origin-name-canada.html

Answer: True [2]

3. True or False? Many Indigenous nations in Canada developed unique combinations of wild plants to relieve coughs, forming what we now know as cough syrup.
Answer: True [3]

4. True or False? Indigenous nations in Canada have been using the main ingredient in aspirin for centuries.
Answer: True [4]

5. Where in Canada is the historic homeland of the Metis?
   a. Winnipeg, Manitoba
   b. Toronto, Ontario
   c. Manitoba, Saskatchewan, and Alberta
   d. Saskatoon, Saskatchewan

Answer: C (Manitoba, Saskatchewan, and Alberta) [5]

6. In what year did the last residential school in Canada close?
   a. 1966
   b. 1976
   c. 1986
   d. 1996

Answer: D (1996) [6]

7. Approximately 150,000 Indigenous children attended Residential Schools. What percentage of these children died there?
   a. 10%
   b. 25%
   c. 50%
   d. 60%

Answer: B (25%) [7]

8. What is an example of a Treaty Right?
   a. The right to hunt and fish on unoccupied Crown land
   b. Resource revenue sharing and measures to participate in the Canadian economy
   c. Schools and teachers on reserves to be paid for by the government
   d. All of the Above [8]

Answer: All of the Above

9. The term Indigenous encompasses...

---

[2] Manitoba Education. "Diverse Peoples – Aboriginal Contributions and Inventions". PDF. https://www.edu.gov.mb.ca/k12/cur/socstud/foundation_gr2/blms/2-2-1c.pdf

[3] Manitoba Education. "Diverse Peoples – Aboriginal Contributions and Inventions". PDF. https://www.edu.gov.mb.ca/k12/cur/socstud/foundation_gr2/blms/2-2-1c.pdf

[4] Manitoba Education. "Diverse Peoples – Aboriginal Contributions and Inventions". PDF. https://www.edu.gov.mb.ca/k12/cur/socstud/foundation_gr2/blms/2-2-1c.pdf

[5] Government of Canada. Metis Nation. Library and Archives Canada. https://www.bac-lac.gc.ca/eng/discover/aboriginal-heritage/metis/Pages/introduction.aspx

[6] Wilson, Kory. Pulling Together: Foundations Guide. BC Campus. https://opentextbc.ca/indigenizationfoundations/

[7] Mosby, Ian & Millions, Erin. "Canada's Residential Schools Were a Horror". Scientific American. 1 August 2021. https://www.scientificamerican.com/article/canadas-residential-schools-were-a-horror/

[8] *Government of Canada.* "Treaties and Agreements". https://www.rcaanc-cirnac.gc.ca/eng/1100100028574/1529354437231

a. Status First Nations
b. Both Status and Non-Status First Nations
c. Fist Nations (Status or Non-Status), Inuit and Metis people in Canada
d. First Nations (Status only), Inuit and Metis people in Canada

Answer: C (Fist Nations [Status or Non-Status], Inuit and Metis people in Canada)

10. How many First Nations are there in Canada? [9]

a. 0-100
b. 100-250
c. 250-500
d. 500+

Answer: D (500+) [10]

Determine which team won the quiz. Ask students what fact surprised them the most. Why was this surprising to them? How many students have learned about Indigenous topics in-depth?

Inform students that next, they will hear from Indigenous educator, Niigaan Sinclair.

ACQUIRE: NIIGAAN SINCLAIR'S FIRESIDE CHAT VIDEO

https://www.firesidechats.ca/video/niigaan-sinclair

Niigaanwewidam James Sinclair is Anishinaabe (St. Peter's/Little Peguis) and an Assistant Professor at the University of Manitoba. He is a regular commentator on Indigenous issues on CTV, CBC, and APTN, and his written work can be found in the pages of The Exile Edition of Native Canadian Fiction and Drama, newspapers like The Guardian, and online with CBC Books: Canada Writes. Niigaan is the co-editor of the award-winning Manitowapow: Aboriginal Writings from the Land of Water (Highwater Press, 2011) and Centering Anishinaabeg Studies: Understanding the World Through Stories (Michigan State University Press, 2013), and is the Editorial Director of The Debwe Series with Portage and Main Press. Niigaan obtained his BA in Education at the University of Winnipeg, before completing an MA in Native- and African-American literatures at the University of Oklahoma, and a PhD in First Nations and American Literatures from the University of British Columbia.

Play Niigaan Sinclair's Fireside Chat Video or read his chapter in the textbook.

To debrief the video, ask the class the following questions:

1. What does Niigaan say about his family's connection to land?
2. What was Niigaan's education journey like?
3. What jobs does Niigaan currently hold?
4. What does Niigaan say his underlying motivation is?
5. What does Niigaan say about informal education?
6. What obstacle has Niigaan faced in his life so far and how does he say he overcame them?
7. What message would Niigaan give to his younger self?
8. What advice does Niigaan give to young people thinking about moving away to pursue a job or university?
9. How does Niigaan say he keeps his mental health in check in times of uncertainty?
10. Where does Niigaan say he draws his inspiration from?

In his interview, Niigaan discusses his work as columnist for the *Winnipeg Free Press*. Inform the class that next, they will have the opportunity to read and respond to one of his articles!

---

[9] Wilson, Kory. *Pulling Together: Foundations Guide*. BC Campus. https://opentextbc.ca/indigenizationfoundations/
[10] Wilson, Kory. *Pulling Together: Foundations Guide*. BC Campus. https://opentextbc.ca/indigenizationfoundations/

APPLY: ARTICLE ANALYSIS

Distribute Niigaan's *Winnipeg Free Press* article "Students or Slaves? Work at Residential Schools Under Fire".

Inform students that this type of article is called an editorial. Editorials are opinion pieces that have the power to change people's understanding of the world, influence public opinion and ultimately lead to meaningful action. [11] Have students read the article either together as a class or individually.

Next, have students analyze the article using the "Article Analysis" worksheet and write a one-page reflection by answering the following prompt:

How has reading this article impacted your understanding of residential schools in Canada? How does this learning connect to other parts of the lesson today (i.e., The quiz and Niigaan's interview)?

Use the "Reflection Rubric" to grade students writing.

ASSESS:

The "Indigenous History Quiz" activity is a form of formative assessment. This activity will enable teachers to assess prior knowledge about Indigenous history in Canada.

The debriefing questions after Niigaan's interview with Fireside Chats is a form of formative assessment. Teachers will be able to check students' comprehension of the topics discussed in the video.

The article response and reflection are a form of summative assessment. Teachers will be able to assess students' writing and connections to other parts of the lesson.

---

[11] Schulten, Katherine. "10 Ways to Teach Argument-Writing with the New York Times". New York Times. 5 October 2017.

STUDENTS OR SLAVES? WORK AT RESIDENTIAL SCHOOLS UNDER FIRE

Report finds egregious examples of 'forced labour and slavery'
By Niigaan Sinclair

Monday, August 9, 2021

Winnipeg Free Press

Ten years ago, I asked my French, non-Native grandmother if she had ever heard of residential schools.

She was born in 1920, and grew up in The Pas. MacKay Indian Residential School was located about 10 kilometres north-west of the Manitoba town, operating from 1914 to 1933, when it was destroyed by fire.

"No," she told me, "but every year, young Indian girls would come door-to-door selling clothes and mitts they had sewn while in school. I remember because they were my age."

According to new findings by Manitoba-based researchers, what she witnessed was evidence of something much worse.

In studying local residential schools (1888-1950), Anne Lindsay (University of Manitoba PhD candidate) and Karlee Sapoznik Evans (in the office of Manitoba advocate for children and youth) have concluded children were forced to perform so much unpaid labour to keep residential schools afloat it constituted slavery.

"As evidenced in the stories of IRS pupils in Manitoba," Lindsay and Sapoznik Evans report, "forced child labour and slavery, framed as 'educational training,' was foundational and central to the residential schools system operated by the Canadian government and churches."

Virtually every residential school was underfunded by the federal government, who had a legal obligation to provide education to First Nations children under treaties. To make up the shortfall, schools ran farms, sewing businesses, and sent children into the community to work, with much of the money going to pay for the operation of the school.

For many, this meant long, hard days doing work under dangerous, often unsupervised, conditions.

Lindsay and Sapoznik Evans found evidence First Nations leaders complained to government agents their children were treated like "labourers" instead of students, and children ran away from schools because they felt they were being worked to death.

During the Truth and Reconciliation Commission of Canada hearings, one survivor of Birtle Indian Residential School, Sam Ross, told commissioners throughout the 1950s he had to work 16-hour days in the barn and boiler room.

When he turned 18, well past the legal age when students could leave the school, Ross asked the principal if he could go home. He was refused.

During the 20th century, government officials increasingly commented this overwhelming amount of labour had little educational value.

While visiting Portage la Prairie in 1943, school inspector Eldon Simms wrote the students spent a large amount of their day working at jobs "which should rightly be done by hired help... The girls are employed largely in scrubbing and the boys in farm chores, and I question the value of this as educational training."

Touring schools throughout northwestern Ontario, Manitoba, and Saskatchewan in 1946, Indian Affairs official A.J. Doucet reported "little organized training is taking place."

Canadians were informed students were suffering like slaves and nothing was done.

Kenneth Thompson ran away from the Brandon residential school in 1936, and told police: "I ran away from school because I have to work too hard, in fact I do not study at all. I am working around the school all the time."

At the Elkhorn residential school, there was a shop that printed the local newspaper, a carpentry business and a boot shop that prepared high-end orders from "many well-known people in the West."

At Norway House, the principal of the residential school petitioned the Department of Indian Affairs to force students to stay until they were 19 because: "(Older students) are able to carry our heavier tasks and so take the place of help that would have to be hired from the outside. The present financial condition of our schools will not allow the engagement of much outside help on current wages."

In some cases, Lindsay and Sapoznik Evans document, child labour provided up to 20 per cent of the funding of a residential school.

This constitutes a model that resembles slavery plantations in the southern U.S. and fully meets the criteria of "forced child labour and slavery," as established in 1920s international law.

By the 1940s, Canadian officials recognized residential schools had little to no education and most had become what the final TRC report called "child labour camps."

As the report stated: "It is clear from the record that rather than being given training that helped them develop employable skills, students spent their half-day doing repetitive chores that helped subsidize school operations."

It not only means the residential school system was evidence of openly practised slavery, but Manitoba's economy was built on this servitude.

Worst of all, many Canadians knew what was happening.

Final proof of this came in 1950, when the federal government mandated residential school students spend full days in the classroom — similar to their Canadian counterparts.

ARTICLE ANALYSIS

Analyze Niigaan's article by filling in the chart below. Complete the final prompt by writing a one-page reflection.

Who (2 marks)
What (2 marks)
When (2 marks)
Where (2 marks)
Why (2 marks)
How (2 marks)
Author's Main Argument (2 marks)
Evidence that Supports Argument (6 marks)

Written Reflection (15 marks; see rubric):

How has reading this article impacted your understanding of residential schools in Canada? How does this learning connect to other parts of the lesson today (i.e., The quiz and Niigaan's interview)?

Total = 35 marks

REFLECTION RUBRIC

	EXCELLENT (5)	GOOD (4)	SATISFACTORY (3-2)	NEEDS IMPROVEMENT (1-0)
Content /5	The author effectively answers the reflection prompts	The author answers the reflection prompts	The author attempts to answer one or more of the reflection prompts	The author does not answer the reflection prompts
Connections /5	The author makes connections between the editorial, other parts of the lesson, personal experience, and prior learning	The author makes connections between the editorial and other parts of the lesson	The author attempts to make connections between the editorial and other parts of the lesson	The author does not attempt to make connections
Analysis /5	The author provides a superior analysis of the editorial and offers multiple viewpoints and insights	The author provides an insightful analysis of the editorial	The author provides a simple description of the editorial and attempts to analyze its contents	No attempt at analysis is made

Total = _____ out of 15

Teacher Comments:

Lesson Four: Dr. Glen Sharpe

Activity: Embracing Failure

CURRICULUM CONNECTIONS	**Alberta, Northwest Territories and Nunavut:** • Aboriginal Studies Grades 10-12 • School Health Program, Grade 9 • Career-Life Management **British Columbia and Yukon:** • Contemporary Indigenous Studies Grade 12 • Physical and Health Education 9 • Physical and Health Education Grade 10 **Ontario:** • First Nations, Metis, and Inuit Studies Grades 9-12 • Health and Physical Education 9-12 • Health and Physical Education Grades 9-12 • Personal Life Management Grade 12 • Dynamics of Human Relationships Grade 11 • Exploring Family Studies Grades 9-10
DURATION	1-2 Hours
OVERVIEW	Throughout this lesson, students will learn about an important concept related to their beliefs about learning and bouncing back from life's setbacks – mindset. Students will first engage in an agree/disagree activity, comparing their personal beliefs about success and failure with the rest of the class. Next, students will listen to Dr. Glen Sharpe's Fireside Chat interview where he talks about his experiences turning moments of failure into learning opportunities. Finally, students will reflect on a time they initially failed at something and then turned it into a learning experience. By reflecting on moments of failure, students will be engaging in meta-cognition and transforming their personal narratives around failure to reflect a growth mindset. Reflections will be graded using a "Reflection Rubric".
MATERIALS	• Computer/Projector/Internet • Paper, Pencils • "Reflection Rubric"

Lesson Plan

☀ ACTIVATE: AGREE/DISAGREE ACTIVITY

To begin this lesson, without giving any context, designate one side of the classroom as the "agree" side, and the opposite side as the "disagree" side. Have students gather in the middle of the class, and when you read out a statement, instruct them to move to the "agree" side if they agree with the statement or the "disagree" side if they disagree with the statement. Inform students there are no right or wrong answers, only personal beliefs.

After students have picked a side, you may want to ask a student from each side to volunteer why they chose the side they did.

Statements:

1. Either I'm good at something or I'm not.
2. There's no point in trying if I'm going to fail.
3. Failure is permanent.
4. Success is permanent.
5. Other peoples' success intimidates me.
6. Learning is a result of failure.
7. Success comes to those who don't give up.
8. Anyone can be successful if they try hard enough.
9. I find it easy to admit I need help.
10. No one is born smart.

Once the activity is done, ask students to raise their hands if they mainly answered "agree" to the first five statements. Inform these students that they have what is referred to as a "fixed mindset".

Ask students to raise their hands if they mainly answered "agree" to the last five statements. Inform these students that they have what is referred to as a "growth mindset".

Inform students that we will explore these concepts of mindset more in the latter half of the lesson but for now, they will hear from Indigenous educator, Dr. Glen Sharpe.

ACQUIRE: DR. GLEN SHARPE'S FIRESIDE CHAT VIDEO

https://www.firesidechats.ca/video/glen-sharpe

Dr. Sharpe completed his BEd at Lakehead University, his MEd at Nipissing University and his EDd at OISE/University of Toronto. Dr. Sharpe's primary research interests include Teacher Abuse of Elementary Aged Students, Bullying, Aboriginal Education, Democratic, and Inclusive Education. Dr. Sharpe is Mohawk of the Bay of Quinte and is actively involved with several Aboriginal Organizations (INDSPIRE as a Teacher Mentor, Aboriginal Professionals Association of Canada, The Aboriginal Circle of Educators and Teach for Canada). In 2012 Dr. Sharpe was awarded Nipissing University's Distinguished Alumni Award. In 2015 Glen was awarded the Researcher Award with The Aboriginal Circle of Educators. The Aboriginal Professionals Association of Canada highlighted Dr. Sharpe's work in their Recognizing Excellence Program in July of 2015. In March 2016, Dr. Sharpe was awarded The Governor General of Canada's Sovereign's Medal for his community engagement. In 2018, Glen was given the Chancellor's Award for Excellence in Teaching from Nipissing University.

Play Dr. Glen Sharpe's Fireside Chat Video or have students read his story in the textbook.

To debrief the video, ask the class the following questions:

1. What was Glen's educational journey like?
2. What does Glen say about his success?
3. What does Glen say was his "aha moment"?
4. How did Glen demonstrate perseverance throughout his life?
5. What obstacles did Glen face and how does he say he overcame them?
6. What does Glen say about his experience leaving home at a young age to attend school? What advice does he give to ease the transition?

In his interview, Dr. Glen Sharpe discusses learning from failure. Inform the class that the next part of the lesson will focus on the concept of mindset.

APPLY: MINDSET AND EMBRACING FAILURE REFLECTION

Inform the class that Dr. Glen Sharpe alludes to an important concept in his Fireside Chat interview – mindset. Inform the class that according to Stanford psychologist, Carol Dweck, people have one of two types of mindsets – fixed or growth. Mindset refers to a person's underlying beliefs about learning and intelligence. [1]

Explain that a person with a fixed mindset believes that intelligence is fixed, or static, meaning it cannot be changed. On the other hand, a person with a growth mindset believes that intelligence can be developed. Carol Dweck's research focuses on how we can transform fixed mindsets to growth mindsets so that people, and in particular – students - can learn to rebound after failure rather than be devastated by small setbacks. [2]

Inform students that their assignment today will be to write about a time they learned from failure. Even if they didn't think of it as a learning experience at the time, how can they make it into a learning experience now? Teachers are encouraged to share a personal example with the class to help get them thinking.

Allow students time to write their reflection. Use the "Reflection Rubric" to grade their writing.

ASSESS:

The "Agree/Disagree" activity is a form of formative assessment. This activity will enable teachers and students to gauge their own and other's personal beliefs about success and failure.

The debriefing questions after Dr. Glen Sharpe's interview with Fireside Chats is a form of formative assessment. Teachers will be able to check students' comprehension of the topics discussed in the video.

The written reflection is a form of summative assessment. Teachers will be able to assess students' writing and connections to other parts of the lesson.

---

[1] "The Impact of a Growth Mindset". Mindsetworks.com. https://www.mindsetworks.com/science/Impact

[2] "Decades of Scientific Research that Started a Growth Mindset Revolution". Mindsetworks.com https://www.mindsetworks.com/science/Default

REFLECTION RUBRIC

Reflection Prompts: *Write about a time you initially failed at something. How did you learn from it? Even if you didn't think of it as a learning experience at the time, how can you make it into a learning experience now?*

	EXCELLENT (5)	GOOD (4)	SATISFACTORY (3-2)	NEEDS IMPROVEMENT (1-0)
Content /5	The author effectively answers the reflection prompts	The author answers the reflection prompts	The author attempts to answer one or more of the reflection prompts	The author does not answer the reflection prompts
Connections /5	The author makes connections between the prompts, other parts of the lesson, personal experience, and prior learning	The author makes connections between the prompts and other parts of the lesson	The author attempts to make connections between the prompts and other parts of the lesson	The author does not attempt to make connections
Depth /5	The author provides an in-depth discussion about mindset, failure, and learning	The author provides an insightful discussion about mindset, failure, and learning	The author provides a simple description of mindset, failure, and learning	No attempt at in-depth reflection is made

Total = _____ out of 15

Teacher Comments:

Lesson One: Diane Roussin

Activity: Creating Social Change

CURRICULUM CONNECTIONS	Alberta, Northwest Territories and Nunavut:
	• Aboriginal Studies Grades 10-12
	• English Language Arts Grades 10-12
	• English Language Arts Grades 10, 11, 12: Uqausiliriniq Strand
	British Columbia and Yukon:
	• Contemporary Indigenous Studies Grade 12
	• English Language Arts Composition Grades 10, 11, 12
	Ontario:
	• First Nations, Metis, and Inuit Studies Grades 9-12
	• English Language Arts Grades 9-10
	• English Language Arts Grades 11-12

DURATION	3-4 Hours

OVERVIEW	Throughout this lesson, students will explore the concept of social change. First, students will engage in a carousel activity where they will move around the room while brainstorming and discussing specific actions people can take to create social change through advocacy, education, fundraising, volunteering, and creating. The hope is by seeing all the actions people can take to create social change, students will feel empowered! Next, students will learn from Indigenous community leader, Diane Roussin, where she talks about her passion for creating social change. Finally, students will work in pairs to complete a case study on Diane Roussin's social change initiative, The Winnipeg Boldness Project, where they will research and analyze one of her community solutions. Students will present on the solution and teachers can use the "Case Study Presentation Rubric" to assess students research and analytical skills.

MATERIALS	• Computer/Projector/Internet
	• Chart Paper and Markers
	• "Creating Social Change: Case Study" worksheet
	• "Case Study Presentation Rubric"

Lesson Plan

☀ ACTIVATE: SOCIAL CHANGE CAROUSEL

To begin, arrange the tables/desks into four stations. Provide a piece of chart paper and several markers at each station. Divide students into four groups and explain that today's lesson is all about ways to create social change.

Inform students that they will have five minutes at each station to brainstorm as many examples as possible of specific actions to create social change through each of the following categories: advocate, educate, fundraise, volunteer and create. For example, to advocate for someone or something, people can write letters to their member of parliament. Or, to educate, people can create a pamphlet about a topic and distribute it to the community. Once the five minutes is up, students will move to the next station, and brainstorm ideas for the next category. Before they begin a new station, instruct students to first read what the previous group wrote to not duplicate their answers.

On the chart paper at each station, write the following ways to create social change:

1. Advocate
2. Educate
3. Fundraise
4. Volunteer
5. Create

Once groups have been at each station, hang the chart paper around the room and have students walk around and view all the answers. The hope is by seeing all the actions people can take to create social change, students should feel empowered!

Inform students that next, they will hear from Indigenous community leader, Diane Roussin.

ACQUIRE: DIANE ROUSSIN'S FIRESIDE CHAT VIDEO

https://www.firesidechats.ca/video/diane-roussin

Diane Roussin is an Anishinaabe community leader passionately committed to the pursuit of mino bimaadiziwin (the good life) for all families and children. Her in-depth knowledge of Indigenous issues and solutions flow directly from her strong sense of identity and worldview. Diane is a proud member of Skownan First Nation, Agowidiiwinan Treaty 2 Territory. She is currently the Project Director of The Winnipeg Boldness Project.

Play Diane Roussin's Fireside Chat Video or have students read the story from the textbook.

To debrief the video, ask the class the following questions:

1. How does Diane describe her childhood?
2. What does Diane do now?
3. Who does Diane say had the biggest impact on her?
4. What advice does Diane give to youth thinking about leaving their home community to go to school?
5. What obstacles has Diane faced and how has she overcome them?
6. What message would Diane give to her younger self?
7. How does Diane say she keeps her mental health in check in times of uncertainty?

In her interview, Diane talks about her community development work through her initiative, the Winnipeg Boldness Project. Inform students they will have the experience to learn more about her initiative in the next part of the lesson.

APPLY: CASE STUDY

Inform students that they are going to use the Winnipeg Boldness Project as a case study for creating social change. A case study is an in-depth examination and analysis of something. In this case, students will be researching and analyzing the Winnipeg Boldness Project including the issues the initiative tackles, as well as the solutions (or prototypes) they came up with.

Hand out the "Creating Social Change Case Study" worksheet and instruct students to work in pairs to complete the research, using the Winnipeg Boldness Project website at www.winnipegboldness.ca.

Assign teams one of the twelve solutions, or, have teams choose the solution of their choice. Note: The website uses the term "prototypes".

1. Indigenous Doula Initiative: Pre and Post Pregnancy Care
2. Baby Basket: Supporting New Parents
3. Health & Wellness Planning: Pregnancy & Family Support

4. Supports for Dads: Increasing Family Togetherness
5. Early Childhood Engagement
6. Hub of Strength: Building Community Capacity and Leadership
7. Transportation: Increasing Neighbourhood Accessibility
8. Housing
9. Natural Support Systems: Connecting Local Residents
10. North End Wellbeing Measure
11. Canada Learning Bond: Growing a College-Bound Identity
12. Participation in the Arts: Providing Inclusive Opportunities for Skill Building

Once students complete their research, they should answer the analysis questions. Finally, students will present on their solution to the class, answering the analysis questions within their presentation.

Use the "Case Study Presentation Rubric" to grade assignments.

ASSESS:

The sticky notes activity is a form of formative assessment. This activity will enable teachers to assess students' prior knowledge.

The debriefing questions after Diane's interview with Fireside Chats is a form of formative assessment. Teachers will be able to check what students took away from the video and make connections to the other parts of the lesson.

The case study is a form of summative assessment. Teachers will be able to assess students research and analytical skills. Teachers can grade the assignment using the "Case Study Rubric".

TAKE LEARNING FURTHER

Watch Diane's TedXWinnipeg talk "Indigenous Social Innovation" at https://tedxwinnipeg.ca/speaker/diane-roussin/ to learn about Indigenous wisdom and reflect on how it can be used to create solutions to tackle big problems in the health, education and justice system in Canada.

Have students research a problem or issue in their communities and then take action using one of the specific actions to create social change discussed in the activating activity - advocate, educate, fundraise, volunteer and create.

CREATING SOCIAL CHANGE: CASE STUDY

Use The Winnipeg Boldness Project website at https://www.winnipegboldness.ca to research the initiative in general, as well as solution you've been assigned. Once you complete your research, answer the analysis questions in paragraph form.

Assigned Solution: _____

The General Problem:
The General Project:
The Team:
The Values:
The Solution:

ANALYSIS QUESTIONS:

1. What could be the indicators of success for the solution?

2. Do you think the solution was successful in creating social change? Why or why not?

3. Could this solution be more effective? How?

4. What is the role of building and maintaining relationships in this case study?

5. What questions do you still have?

CASE STUDY PRESENTATION RUBRIC

	EXCELLENT (5)	GOOD (4)	SATISFACTORY (3-2)	NEEDS IMPROVEMENT (1-0)
Content /10	The problem and solution are effectively described	The problem and solution are described	An overview of the problem and solution are given	The problem and solution are not described
Analysis /10	The solution is thoroughly analyzed and the presenters include thoughtful answers to all the questions	The solution is analyzed and the presenters include thoughtful answers to most of the questions	The solution is somewhat analyzed and the presenters attempt to answer the questions	No attempt at anlayzing the solution or answering the questions is made
Presentation /5	The presenters maintain eye contact, appropriate tone of voice and confident body language throughout the presentation	The presenters mostly maintain eye contact, appropriate tone of voice and confident body language throughout the presentation	The presenters attempt to maintain eye contact, appropriate tone of voice and confident body language throughout the presentation	The presenters do not maintain eye contact, appropriate tone of voice and confident body language throughout the presentation

Total = _____ out of 25

Teacher Comments:

Lesson Two: Reanna Merasty
Activity: Indigenous Architecture

CURRICULUM CONNECTIONS	**Alberta, Northwest Territories and Nunavut:** • Aboriginal Studies Grades 10-12 • English Language Arts Grades 10-12 • English Language Arts Grades 10, 11, 12: Uqausiliriniq Strand **British Columbia and Yukon:** • Contemporary Indigenous Studies Grade 12 • English Language Arts Composition Grades 10, 11, 12. **Ontario:** • First Nations, Metis, and Inuit Studies Grades 9-12 • English Language Arts Grades 9-10 • English Language Arts Grades 11-12
DURATION	1-2 Hours
OVERVIEW	Throughout this lesson, students will be introduced to the topic of Indigenous architecture. First, students will access their prior knowledge about the topic by complete the first two sections of a "K/W/L Chart". Then, students will listen to Reanna Merasty's Fireside Chat interview where she discusses her educational journey becoming an architect. Next, students will read one of Reanna's published articles titled "Leadership in Architecture and Land-Based Practices" which was published in Say Magazine. Students will then engage in small group discussions to debrief the article. Finally, students will complete the final section of their "K/W/L Chart" handout.
MATERIALS	• Computer/Projector/Internet • "K/W/L Chart" handout • "Leadership in Architecture and Land-Based Practices" Article

Lesson Plan

✳ ACTIVATE: K/W/L CHART

To begin the lesson, hand out the "K/W/L" chart and inform students the topic they will be writing about is "Indigenous Architecture". Have students write everything they know about Indigenous architecture in the "Know" section. Then, have students write everything they want to know in the "Want to Know" section. Students will fill out the last section at the end of the lesson.

Inform students that next, they will hear from Indigenous architect student, Reanna Merasty.

ACQUIRE: REANNA MERASTY'S FIRESIDE CHAT VIDEO

https://www.firesidechats.ca/video/reanna-merasty

Reanna Merasty is Woodlands Cree and is a member of Barren Lands First Nation. She is currently pursuing a Master of Architecture at the University of Manitoba (UofM) and holds a Bachelor of Environmental Design. Reanna works as a Student Intern/Designer at Brook McIlroy in their Indigenous Design Studio, is the Co-Founder/Chair of the Indigenous Design & Planning Students Association at the UofM, and a Research Assistant for several First Nation housing initiatives such as the Mino Bimaadiziwin Partnership, and One House Many Nations.

Play Reanna Merasty's Fireside Chat Video or have students read her story in the textbook.

To debrief the video, ask the class the following questions:

1. What does Reanna do for work?
2. What does Reanna say motivated her to get into architecture?
3. What is the process to become an architect?
4. What obstacles has Reanna faced and how has she overcome them?
5. What does Reanna say about mental health and how does she keep hers in check?
6. What does Reanna say inspires her?

In her interview, Reanna talks about her passion for Indigenous architecture. Inform the class that next, they will have the opportunity to read one of Reanna's published articles.

APPLY: "LEADERSHIP IN ARCHITECTURE AND LAND-BASED PRACTICES" DISCUSSION

Distribute the "Leadership in Architecture and Land-Based Practices" article authored by Reanna Merasty.

Have students read the article individually or read it together as a class.

Next, divide students into small groups of 3-4 to engage in small group discussions. Inform them that you are going to give them 2-3 minutes to answer each question (there are six). After the 2-3 minutes is up, solicit groups to summarize what they talked about with the rest of the class.

1. What is your biggest take-away from today's lesson?
2. Have you ever been into an "Indigenized" space? If so, describe it.
3. Which of Reanna's seven Indigenous design principles resonated with you the most and why?
4. How is Indigenous architecture different from the architecture around us today?
5. What questions do you still have about Indigenous architecture?
6. Would you be interested in a career in architecture? Why or why not?

Finally, instruct students to complete the "Learned" section of their K/W/L charts.

ASSESS:

The "K" and "W" part of the K/W/L chart is a form of formative assessment. This activity will enable teachers to assess students' prior knowledge and interest in the subject of Indigenous architecture.

The debriefing questions after Reanna's interview with Fireside Chats is a form of formative assessment. Teachers will be able to check what students took away from the video and make connections to the other parts of the lesson.

The small group discussions are a form of formative assessment. Teachers can determine what students took away from the article as well as the connections made to other parts of the lesson.

The "L" section of the K/W/L chart is a form of summative assessment. Teachers have the option of assigning grade points for each piece of information learned.

K/W/L CHART

Topic: Indigenous Architecture

Prior to the lesson, fill in the "K" section with everything you know about topic, and the "W" section with everything you want to know. At the end of the lesson, you will fill in the "L" section with everything you learned about the topic.

Know	Want to Know	Learned

LEADERSHIP IN ARCHITECTURE AND LAND-BASED PRACTICES

Say Magazine
12 Jun 2021

By Reanna Merasty

Creativity is an extension of our being, and a reflection of the land that raised and surrounds us. My upbringing was in the North, practicing the traditions of my Nîhithaw (Woodlands Cree) ancestors, practices that take form through craft, construction and methods of retrieving food from the land. I lived on an island surrounding the clear body of water of Reindeer Lake (Northern Manitoba), neighbouring my home community of Barren Lands First Nation.

Render of gathering space, Indigenous Education Transition Centre, 2019

My earliest recollection of creating was alongside my mooshum (grandpa), who has practiced the craft of building his entire life, taught by his father, and his father before him. Often, I picture him walking through a forest with his keen eye for analyzing the trees. I picture sitting on top of logs on our boat as we transfer the trees from island to island and the shavings of birch bark as I help strip each piece for construction. My upbringing sparked a passion in me, not to only build for our people, but to create something that truly honours and contributes to the flourishing of the natural environment.

Architecture, in my view, has become disconnected from its surroundings and is an alienated mass on the natural, contributing to the degradation of the environment, offering little positive output. As a response, we must create spaces that not only reflect the landscape on which it resides but also reflects the health of our surroundings. This reflects the values and practices of our ancestors who looked to the environment for solutions and understood the strength of each element. They allowed the ecology and other living beings to lead and dictate what they created.

When I create, I directly embed the values and principles of my experiences on Reindeer Lake, of my ancestors and as an Indigenous woman. This has influenced my own seven guiding design principles that I use to ground myself and the creation of architectural spaces.

First, honour the land and site where you want to create, connecting with the existing, being good with your intentions and listening to their stories. Practice humility, understanding that the land is greater than us and we depend greatly on her; she requires reverence. Allow the land to lead as design solutions start with place, for they've survived for thousands of years and adhere to the climate and environment intuitively. Tread lightly and gently as you work with the land beneath you and around you. Make the living energies of the land present and showcase their connections in a web of relationships. Practice reciprocal actions, giving back more than you take, assuring the land is impacted positively. Finally, create with a good/kind heart and mind, and apply heart-work.

Architecture requires representation and influence of lands and traditions in its construction and how it meaningfully impacts the surrounding environment. Since time immemorial, our practices as Indigenous Peoples have intertwined with the natural—positively impacting the living world that sustains us, in its health and wellness. The land offers us solutions to degradation. We just have to let it lead in our built environment.

Reanna Merasty (Cree, Barren Lands First Nation) is the co-founder of the Indigenous Design and Planning Student Association at the University of Manitoba (UofM), where she advocates for representation and inclusion in design education. She is also the co-editor of the publication Voices of the Land: Indigenous Design and Planning from the Prairies. Merasty is a M.Arch candidate at the UofM and an architectural intern, focusing on reciprocity and land-based pedagogy.

Render of East Lookout, Pritchard's Creek Healing Centre, 2020 South section

Manufactured by Amazon.ca
Bolton, ON

29910081R00114